YES I CAN!

Interdisciplinary Activities That Promote Success

Written by

Floretta Latham, BA, SLP

Amy Baad, OTR, MA

Christina Cooper, PT, MPA

Illustrated by Mary Rojas

Teaching & Learning Company

1204 Buchanan St., P.O. Box 10
Carthage, IL 62321-0010

This book belongs to

_____

To the many children who have inspired us with their uniqueness, and
challenged us to create an environment where everyone could learn and succeed.
They have forever warmed our hearts with shouts of "YES I CAN!"

Special thanks to the teachers, professionals and parents
for helping to make this program such a success.

And abundant thanks to our husbands,
Dick, Derek and David for their loving support.

Several of the activities in this book involve preparing, tasting
and sharing food items. We urge you to be aware of any food
allergies or restrictions your students may have and to super-
vise these activities diligently. All food-related suggestions
are identified with this allergy-alert symbol: ⚠

Please note: small food items (candies, raisins, cereal, etc.)
can also pose a choking hazard.

Table of Contents

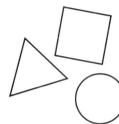
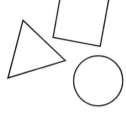

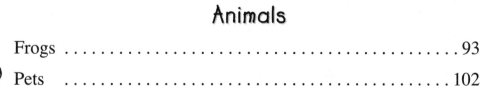

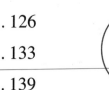

Dear Teacher or Parent,

This book, which is based on the YES I CAN! program, is designed to provide theme-based group activities for children ages three to six years with varying skill levels. It can also be used for older children whose skills are developing in the three- to six-year range. The activities are intended for use by teachers, therapists, paraprofessionals, daycare providers, parents, grandparents and other caregivers. The emphasis is on ability, and the activities can easily be adapted for those with special needs. The ideas presented in this book can be utilized to:

- create a group program using the YES I CAN! model
- select specific themes and activities for use with classrooms or small groups
- select specific activities for use with individuals in a variety of settings

The book is organized in five parts. Each major part, or category, includes three to four themes. For example, in the Seasons category there are three themes: Fall, Winter and Spring. Each of these themes includes five activities.

High-quality, skill-building activities address key developmental areas in the fine motor, visual perceptual motor, gross motor, sensory motor, oral motor, communication and self-care domains. Examples of specific skills addressed include:

- **Fine Motor:** grasp and prehension, cutting, pasting, finger isolation, tracing, copying
- **Visual Perceptual Motor:** visual memory, visual sequencing, parts-to-whole, eye-hand coordination
- **Gross Motor:** mobility, balance and coordination, strength and agility, timed precision, motor planning
- **Sensory Motor:** sensory processing (touch, taste, smell, auditory, visual), "heavy work"
- **Oral Motor:** sucking, swallowing, puckering, blowing
- **Communication:** language comprehension, expressing needs and ideas, following simple and complex directions, auditory memory, vocabulary, articulation, concept development
- **Self-Care:** dressing, undressing, eating, grooming

Whatever your involvement with young children, we encourage you to try some of these ideas. Modify them for each unique child. Make it your mission to teach from your heart. And when you ask them if they can do all these things, listen for that inspired response, "YES I CAN!"

Sincerely,

Floretta, Amy & Christina

Introduction

This book was written by an interdisciplinary team of early childhood professionals representing the fields of speech therapy, occupational therapy and physical therapy. It has grown out of five years of working collaboratively in a program which we call YES I CAN!

The YES I CAN! program is designed to provide theme-based, developmentally appropriate and challenging activities in several key domains—fine motor, visual perceptual motor, gross motor, sensory motor, oral motor, communication and self-care—to a large and diverse group of children ages three to six years with all levels of ability. The strength of the program is that children experience the theme through several modes of learning: auditory, visual, motor and sensory. The program uses a highly motivating and unique group setting model, engages the teaching and paraprofessional staff and involves parents by providing information and suggestions for home activities each time the group convenes.

Each session is planned around a theme that has five theme-based activity centers. Each center focuses on a specific skill area. At the beginning of each session, the children and staff are convened for an overview of the activities. The children are then divided into five small groups, staff is assigned to each group, and they rotate through the activity centers at timed intervals. Teachers, ancillary staff and paraprofessionals assist the children at each center. The children learn new developmental skills, turn-taking, teamwork and sharing in an environment designed to build confidence and self-esteem. At the end of the session, the activities are reviewed, and the children are asked, "If anybody asks you if you can do all of these things, what will you say?" They reply together with a resounding "YES I CAN!"

Parent involvement is encouraged. Parents receive a letter after each weekly session describing the theme and the activity centers. They are encouraged to reinforce the concepts and skills in the home setting to maximize the child's mastery of them. The parents support the program by contributing soft drink cans throughout the year to raise funds for YES I CAN! T-shirts for all of the children.

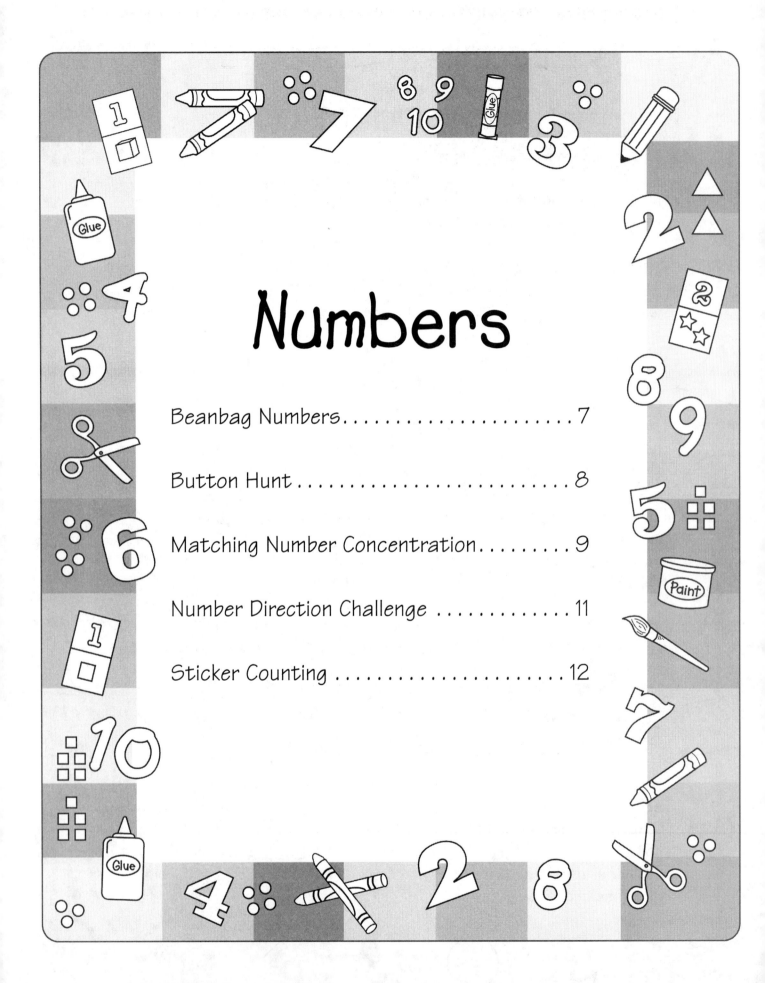

Numbers

TLC10470 Copyright © Teaching & Learning Company, Carthage, IL 62321-0010

Beanbag Numbers

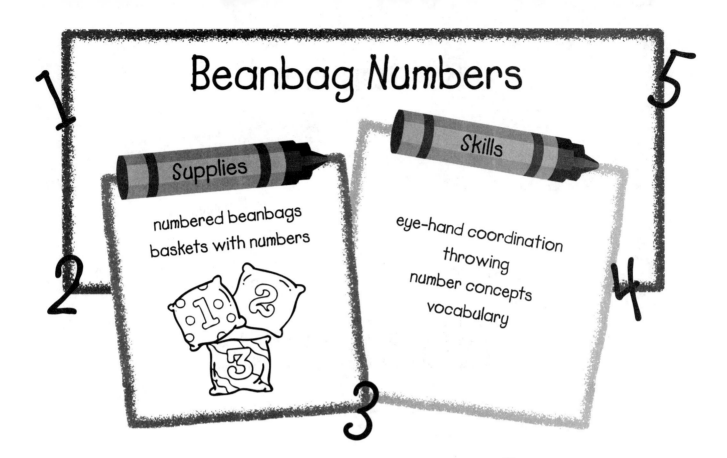

Supplies

numbered beanbags
baskets with numbers

Skills

eye-hand coordination
throwing
number concepts
vocabulary

Instructions for Teacher

Spread the numbered beanbags and baskets out on the floor.

Instructions for Child

1. Pick up a numbered beanbag and say the number aloud.
2. Visually locate the container with the corresponding number on the beanbag and say the number on the container aloud.
3. Wait for the teacher to say whether to throw the beanbag overhand or underhand, then throw the beanbag into the container.
4. Name the basket number in which the beanbag landed.

Variations

Use letters, colors, shapes and pictures instead of numbers.

Button Hunt

Supplies

variety of buttons
scooter boards
plastic cups
traffic cones
colored tape

Skills

bilateral skills
eye-hand coordination
dexterity
strengthening
counting
number concepts
vocabulary

Instructions for Teacher

1. Choose a starting point, then create a course using colored tape as the "path" and cones as obstacles. The tape provides a visual guide for the course to be followed. Along the way, place varied amounts of buttons under plastic cups.
2. Place scooter boards at the starting point.
3. At the end of the session, lift up the cups and count aloud the total number of buttons on the floor.

Instructions for Child

1. Go to the starting point, take a scooter board and lie on your tummy on it.
2. Use your hands to move through the obstacle course.
3. Follow the tape and stop at each of the plastic cups, lifting it up and counting aloud the number of buttons under it.

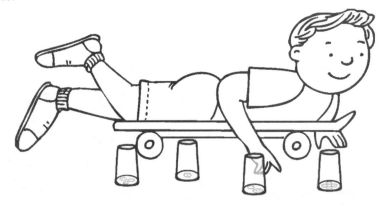

Matching Number Concentration

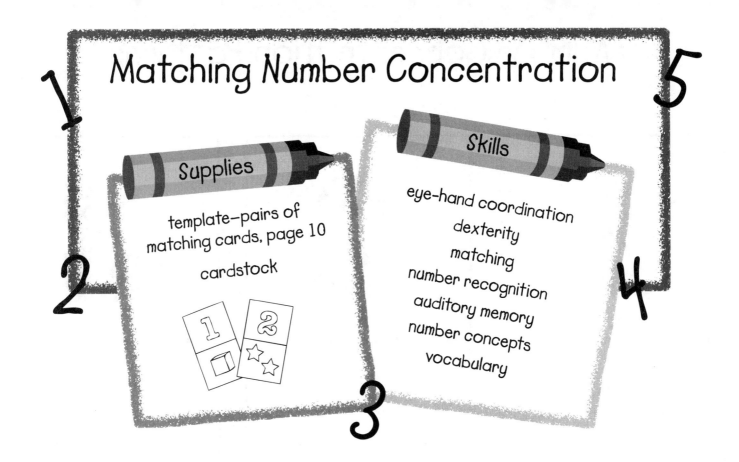

Supplies

template—pairs of matching cards, page 10

cardstock

Skills

eye-hand coordination
dexterity
matching
number recognition
auditory memory
number concepts
vocabulary

Instructions for Teacher

1. Prepare the matching card templates using cardstock paper. Laminate them.
2. Give the child a select number of matching cards (number determined by skill of child).

Instructions for Child

1. Lay the cards on the table, facedown, so that none is touching another.
2. Turn over two cards. Tell what number is on each (if not sure of the number, count the objects).
3. Tell the teacher if the numbers are the same or different.
4. If the numbers are the same, put the cards in a pile off to the side. If they are different, turn the cards back over, remembering where they were.
5. Continue playing the game until all the numbers are matched.

Variations

Use letters, colors, animals or shapes. This game can be played individually or with a partner.

Number Concentration Patterns

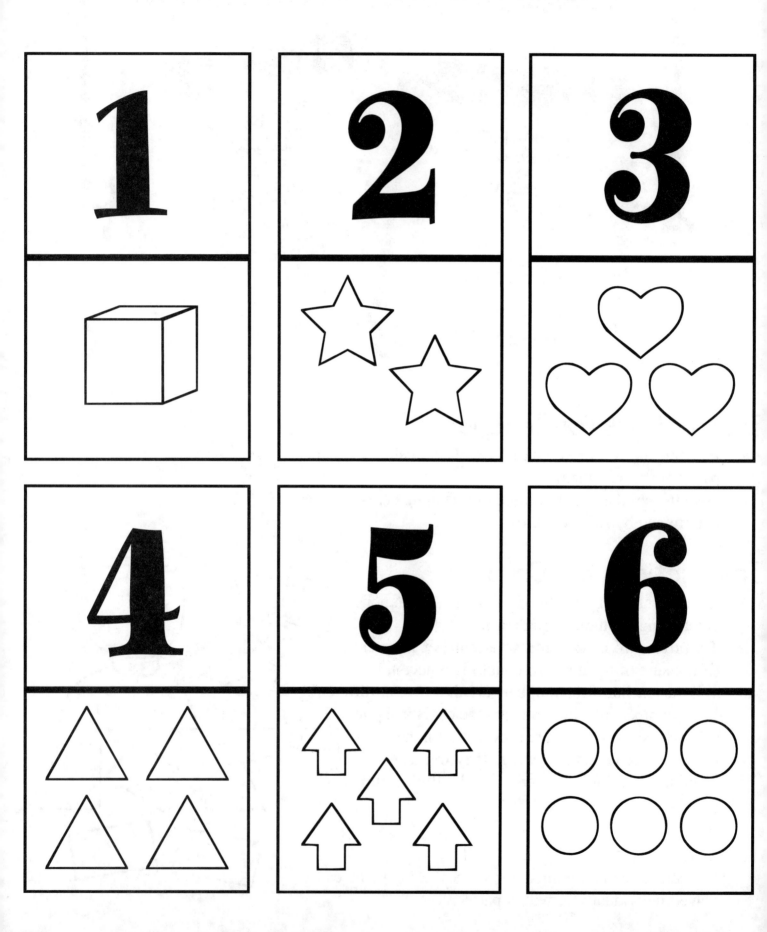

Pre-Readiness Concepts

Number Direction Challenge

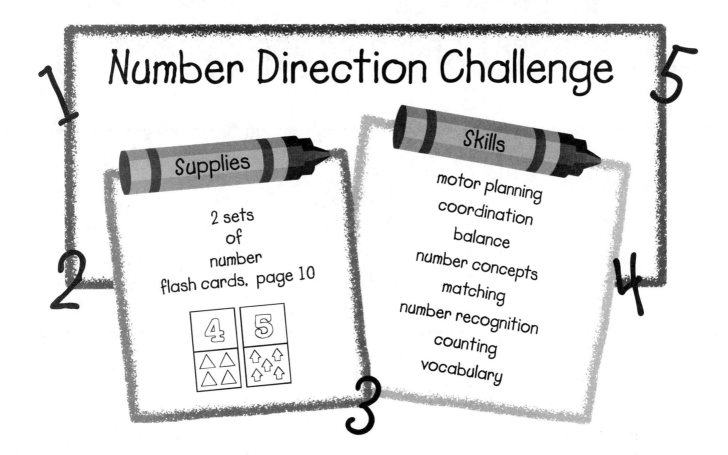

Supplies

2 sets
of
number
flash cards, page 10

Skills

motor planning
coordination
balance
number concepts
matching
number recognition
counting
vocabulary

Instructions for Teacher

1. Place one set of number flash cards faceup on the floor.
2. From the second set of flash cards select a card and show it to the child.

Instructions for Child

1. Name the number the teacher is holding up and find the matching number on the floor.
2. Listen to the teacher for a task using that number: hop three times, take five steps backwards, side step two times, do one somersault, clap hands six times, etc. Do the task.
3. Count aloud as you perform the task.

Sticker Counting

Supplies

template—sticker sheet, page 13
stickers

1 2

Skills

eye-hand coordination
bilateral skills
dexterity
object number correspondence
number concepts
vocabulary

Instructions for Teacher

1. Copy one sticker template sheet for each child and one for a model.
2. Decide if the child will do this activity sitting at a table, lying on the tummy or propped-up on forearms on the floor.
3. Place the sticker sheet and stickers on the table or floor.

Instructions for Child

1. Look at the number in the circle and name it.
2. Select that number of stickers and place them in the circle. (Example: four stickers in the circle labeled four)
3. Count aloud the number of stickers in each circle.

Variations

Use higher numbers in the circles or use shapes or letters instead of numbers. Use a rubber stamp and ink pad instead of stickers.

Sticker Sheet

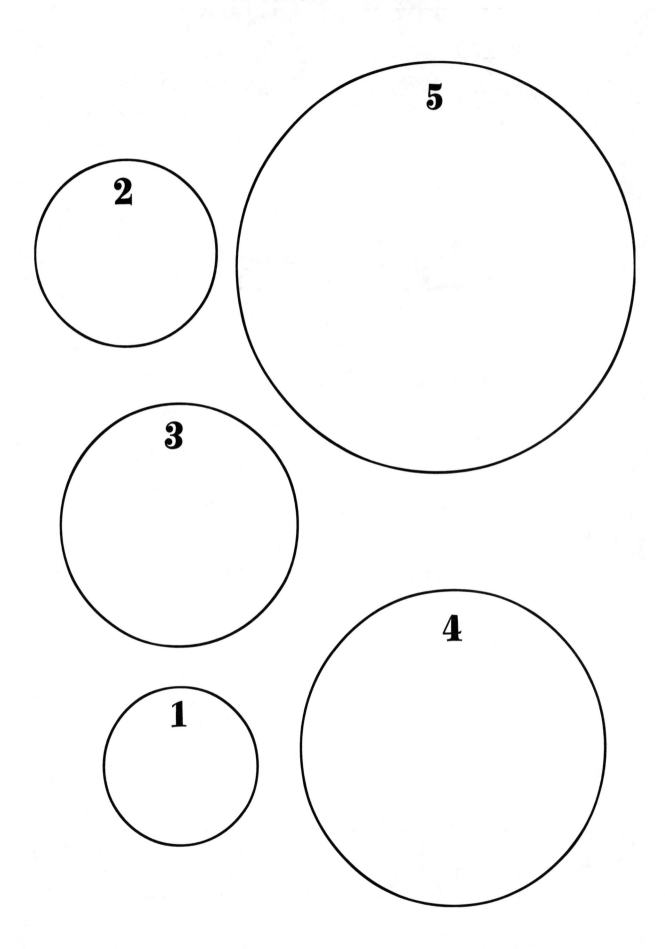

Letters

TLC10470 Copyright © Teaching & Learning Company, Carthage, IL 62321-0010

Letter Sun Catchers

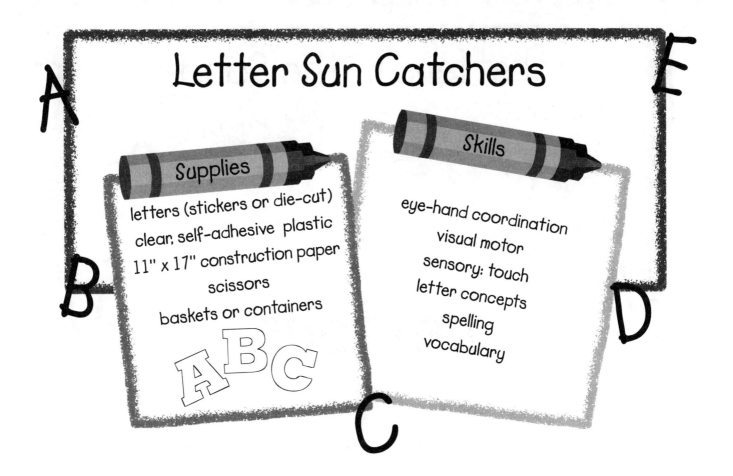

Supplies
letters (stickers or die-cut)
clear, self-adhesive plastic
11" x 17" construction paper
scissors
baskets or containers

Skills
eye-hand coordination
visual motor
sensory: touch
letter concepts
spelling
vocabulary

Instructions for Teacher

1. Cut out a large letter O from 11" x 17" construction paper for each child.
2. Cut out clear, self-adhesive plastic to fit on the letter O for each child.
3. Put the letter stickers or die-cuts in baskets.

Instructions for Child

1. Peel the backing from the sticky paper with a teacher's help and put it on the letter O.
2. Turn the letter over so the sticky side is facing up. Try not to touch it.
3. Put letters on the sticky part of the plastic.
4. Peel the backing off another piece of plastic and have the teacher help you put it over the letters.
5. Take the O to a window to see the beautiful sun catcher in action.

Variations

Have the children spell their names in the Os.

Letters in the Sand

Supplies

visual model of the alphabet

trays (lunch trays or cookie sheets with sides)

sand

cornmeal

dried instant potato flakes

oatmeal

Skills

eye-hand coordination

visual memory

sensory: touch, smell

copying

visual motor skills

letter concepts

vocabulary

Instructions for Teacher

1. Set up a tray with each of the following textured substances: sand, cornmeal, dried instant potato flakes and oatmeal. Place the trays on tables.
2. Display a visual model of the alphabet for the child.
3. Demonstrate how to use an index finger to make letters in the various textures.

Instructions for Child

1. Sit at the table with a texture tray. Put your first finger into the tray and write letters in the texture.
2. Name the letters you made. Move to the next texture tray. Make more letters and name them. Take a turn at each tray.

Variations

Make shapes in the textures. Use different textures such as shaving cream, whipped cream or pudding.

Alphabet Cereal

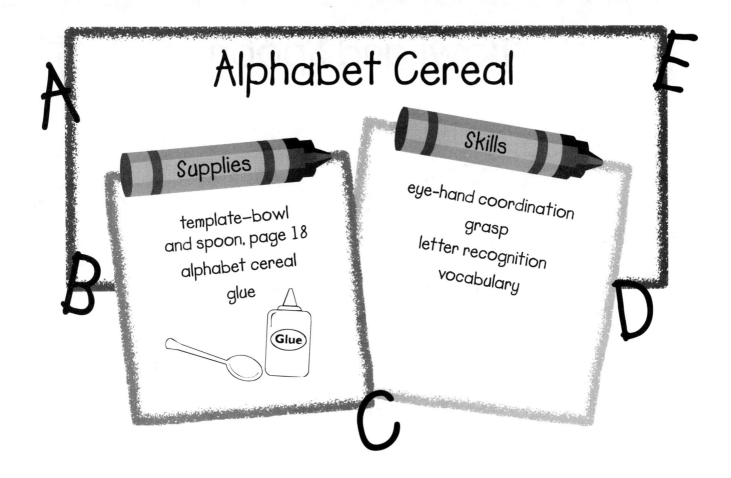

Supplies

template–bowl and spoon, page 18
alphabet cereal
glue

Skills

eye-hand coordination
grasp
letter recognition
vocabulary

Instructions for Teacher

1. Prepare one template of the bowl and spoon for each child.
2. Put the alphabet cereal in a container and place it and the glue on the table.

Instructions for Child

1. Take some alphabet cereal.
2. Glue the letters onto the paper bowl, creating a bowl of alphabet cereal.
3. Name the letters that are glued on your cereal bowl.

Variations

Spell different words or the child's name. For example, the child could work on words that begin with the letter of the day. Visuals may be helpful to assist the child.

Bowl and Spoon

Pre-Readiness Concepts

Letter Cone Ring Toss

Supplies

traffic cones

die-cut letters

masking tape

rings—Rings can be made by cutting the centers out of large, soft plastic lids (margarine tubs, ice cream, etc.).

Skills

eye-hand coordination

motor planning

visual memory

letter concept

vocabulary

Instructions for Teacher

1. Tape a single large letter on each of several cones.
2. Arrange cones in a row.
3. Place a tape line on the floor three to four feet from the cones.

Instructions for Child

1. Pick up a ring and stand on the tape line.
2. Look at all the cones and find the cone with the letter the teacher names.
3. Throw your ring around that cone.
4. Tell the teacher what letter is on the cone your ring is on or near.

Variations

Use cones with numbers, shapes, animals, etc.

Celebrate "Me"

A **E**

Supplies
index cards

die-cut letters of various colors (enough to spell each child's name)

1 9" x 3' sheet of paper for each child

glue

glitter

markers

CD player/marching music

B **C** **D**

Skills
letter recognition

spelling

pasting

sequencing

letter concepts

vocabulary

Instructions for Teacher

1. Prepare a card with each child's name on it.
2. Cut out enough letters so all the children will be able to spell their names.
3. Put the letters, decorations and glue on a table.
4. Cut paper into a 9" x 3' sheet for each child.

Instructions for Child

1. Take your name card, go to the table and find the letters in your name.
2. Arrange the letters on your "banner" so they spell your name.
3. Glue the letters on.
4. Decorate the banner.
5. Line up and march around the room waving your banner in celebration of who you are.

Variations

Count the number of letters in your name. Decide who has the longest/shortest name.

Kera

Colors

Color Walk

red
blue
orange
purple
yellow

Supplies
8½" x 11" construction paper (laminated)— multiple colors
CD player with lively music
masking tape

Skills
motor planning
auditory processing
coordination
following directions
answering questions
color concepts
vocabulary

Instructions for Teacher
1. Tape colored pieces of laminated construction paper in a circle on the floor. Arrange them close enough together so children can step easily from one to another.
2. Place the CD player with lively music close to the circle. Play the music, stopping it intermittently.

Instructions for Child
1. Stand on a colored square of paper.
2. Start walking around the circle when the music begins, stepping on the colors of paper.
3. When the music stops playing, stop and name the color you are standing on.

Variations
Walk backwards, hop, skip, name something the same color as the square being stood on or ask if children are wearing something that matches the color of the square.

Color Relay

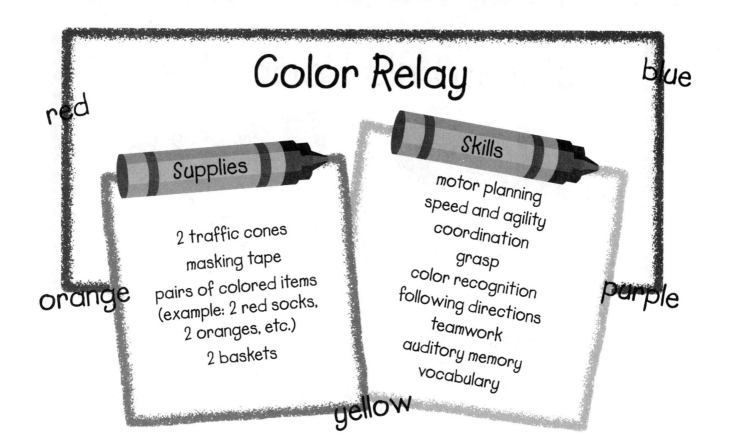

red · blue · orange · purple · yellow

Supplies

2 traffic cones
masking tape
pairs of colored items
(example: 2 red socks,
2 oranges, etc.)
2 baskets

Skills

motor planning
speed and agility
coordination
grasp
color recognition
following directions
teamwork
auditory memory
vocabulary

Instructions for Teacher

1. Put two rows of tape parallel to one another on the floor approximately six feet apart (the length of tape is determined by the number of children).
2. Set a starting point for each team at the end of each tape line. Place a cone for each team 25 to 30 feet from the starting point.
3. Divide the colored items into baskets. Put a basket beside each team's starting point.
4. Divide the children into two teams and have them line up on the tape.
5. Have the first child on each team move to the starting point to begin the relay. Continue until every child on each team has had a turn.

Instructions for Child

1. Listen for the teacher to name a color, then search in the basket for an item of that color.
2. Pick up the item, run around the cone and return to your starting point.
3. Tell the name of the item and put it back in the basket. Then move to the back of the line.
4. The next child in line takes a turn.

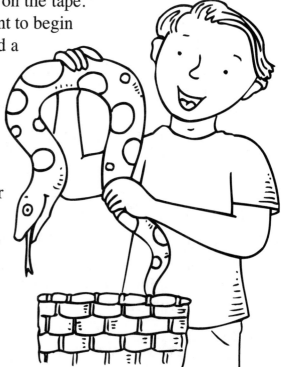

Variations

Walk backwards, hop, skip or pick up two colored items.

Colored Hula Hoop Throw

red   blue

Supplies

colored beanbags
colored Hula Hoops™

Skills

motor planning
grasp
eye-hand coordination
throwing
color concepts
following directions
auditory memory
vocabulary

orange   purple

yellow

Instructions for Teacher

1. Hang three colored Hula Hoops™ from the ceiling or from a basketball hoop. (If this is not possible, lay them on the floor.)

2. Mark a spot on the floor for the child to stand a few feet away from the Hula Hoops™. Place the colored beanbags beside it.

3. Tell the child what color beanbag to pick up, what color hoop to throw it through and whether to throw it overhand or underhand. (Example: "Pick up a blue beanbag and throw it underhand through the red Hula Hoop™.")

Instructions for Child

1. Stand on the spot next to the beanbags.

2. Pick up a (color) beanbag and throw it (overhand/underhand) through the (color) Hula Hoop™.

Color Challenge

red   blue   orange   purple   yellow

Supplies

variety of large shapes cut from tagboard

objects of choice (silverware, stuffed animals, toys, etc.)

Skills

motor planning
following directions
auditory sequential memory
prepositional concepts
color concepts
vocabulary

Instructions for Teacher

1. Place colored tagboard shapes on the floor.
2. Place the objects on the floor in an area a few feet away from the colored shapes.
3. Have children name the shapes, colors and objects.
4. Give simple directions for activities that involve the colored shapes and objects, emphasizing prepositional and color concepts. (Examples: "Susie, put the spoon under the green triangle." "Kera, put the truck beside the orange circle.")

Instructions for Child

1. Name the colors, shapes and objects.
2. Listen and follow the directions of the teacher.

Variations

Use more complex, multi-step directions ("Mary, pick up the car, give it to John and ask him to put it on the purple triangle.")

My Rainbow

red

blue

orange

purple

yellow

Supplies

3-foot piece of butcher paper

crayons or markers

masking tape

stickers

Skills

motor planning

coordination

crossing mid-line

following directions

color concepts

vocabulary

Instructions for Teacher

1. Cut a three-foot piece of roll paper for each child.
2. Tape each child's piece of paper to the floor.
3. Place a sticker in each bottom corner of the paper.
4. Place markers or crayons in a basket close to the paper.
5. Demonstrate how to sit with legs folded and crossed (like a pretzel) on the paper near the back edge.

Instructions for Child

1. Sit on the paper with your legs folded.
2. Find the sticker on either side of you on the paper. Hold your marker on one of the stickers and draw a half circle to the other sticker.
3. Use different colors of markers to draw more half circles until you have a rainbow. Can you name all the colors in your rainbow?

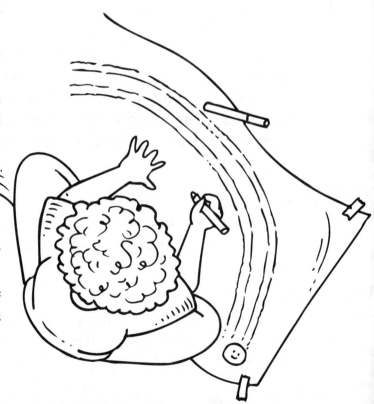

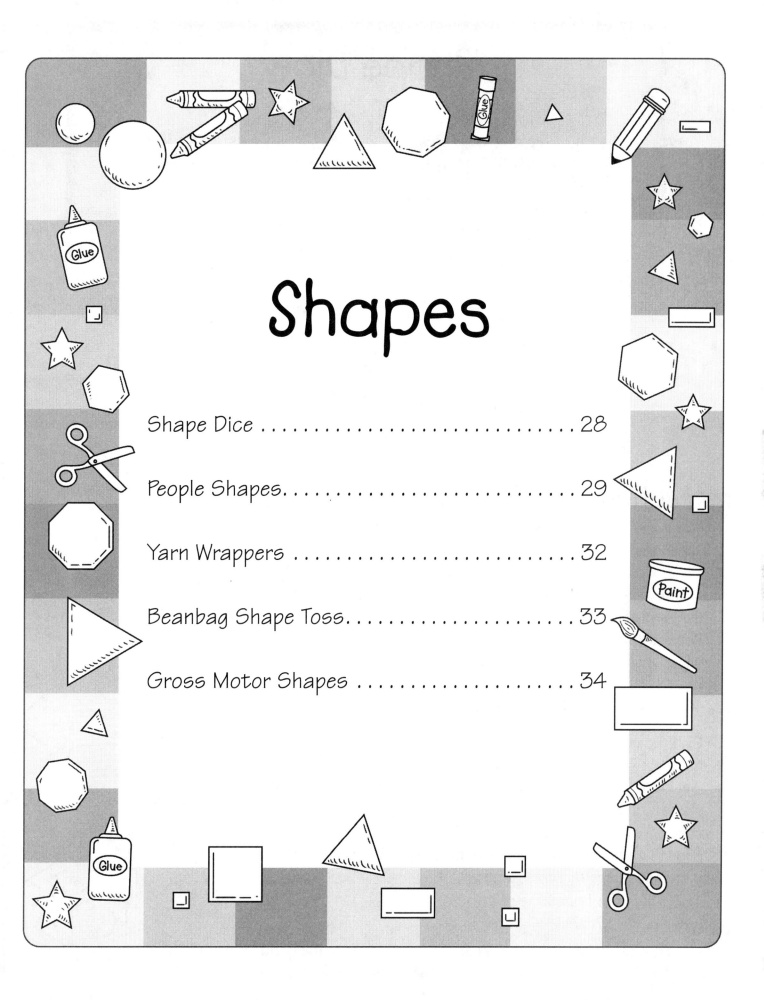

Shapes

Shape Dice

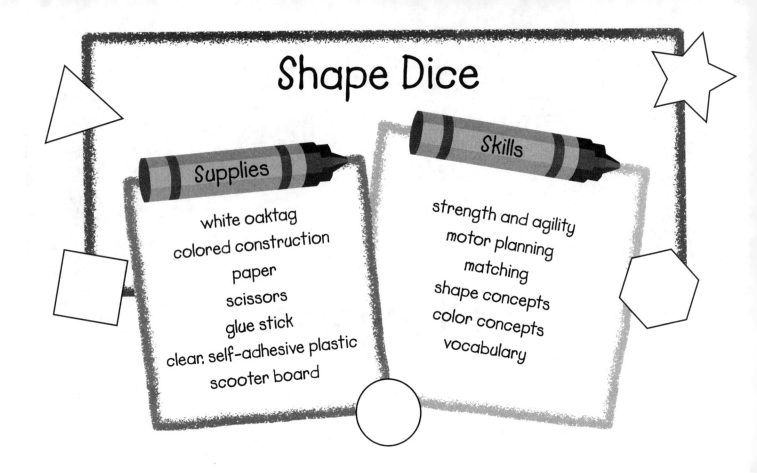

Supplies

white oaktag
colored construction
paper
scissors
glue stick
clear, self-adhesive plastic
scooter board

Skills

strength and agility
motor planning
matching
shape concepts
color concepts
vocabulary

Instructions for Teacher

1. Make a six-inch cube using white oaktag.
2. Glue a small colored construction paper shape on each side of the cube. (Examples: a red circle, a blue square, a green triangle, a yellow rectangle, etc.) Cover the cube with clear, self-adhesive plastic for durability.
3. Set a starting point. Place matching colored construction paper shapes 30 feet from there on the floor.

Instructions for Child

1. Roll the cube on the floor and tell what shape and color is on the top.
2. Get on your tummy on the scooter board, ride to the paper shapes, pick up the shape that is the same as the one on your cube.
3. Ride the scooter board back to the starting point and show the matching shape to your friends.

Variations

Glue multiple shapes on each side of the cube. Have the child find the corresponding number of shapes of the same color.

People Shapes

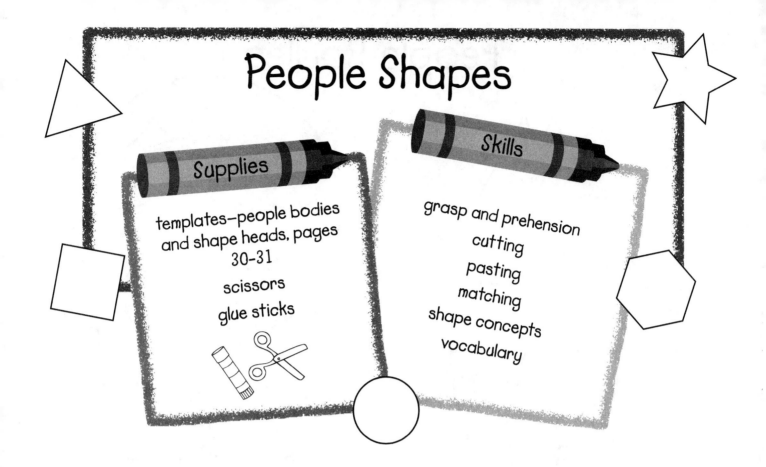

Supplies

templates—people bodies and shape heads, pages 30-31

scissors

glue sticks

Skills

grasp and prehension
cutting
pasting
matching
shape concepts
vocabulary

Instructions for Teacher

1. Make copies of the templates for each child and for a model.
2. Prepare the model by cutting out the head shapes and gluing them on the bodies.
3. Give each child a copy of the templates, scissors and a glue stick.

Instructions for Child

1. Sit at the table and look at the people shapes.
2. Look at the teacher sample. Make one that looks the same.
3. Cut out each head shape and glue it on the body with the same shape.
4. Name each shape as you glue it on.

People Bodies

Pre-Readiness Concepts

Shape Heads

Yarn Wrappers

Supplies

4 24" square pieces
of cardboard
empty thread spools
glue
yarn
carpet squares

Skills

eye-hand coordination
large arm movements
motor planning
sensory processing
shape concepts
vocabulary

Instructions for Teacher

1. Cut a large shape from each piece of cardboard: circle, square, triangle and rectangle. The square should measure approximately 24 inches on each side.
2. Glue empty thread spools along the border of each shape several inches apart. Make sure there is a spool in the corner of each angular shape.
3. Cut a piece of yarn for each shape, long enough so the child can wrap it around the shape several times.
4. Demonstrate how to wrap the yarn around the outside of the spools to make the shape.
5. Give each child a large shape and some yarn.
6. Have each child take a turn with each shape.

Instructions for Child

1. Kneel on a carpet square on the floor.
2. Wrap the yarn around the spools on the large shape.
3. Name your shape.

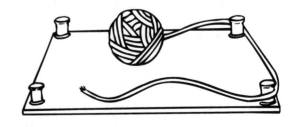

Beanbag Shape Toss

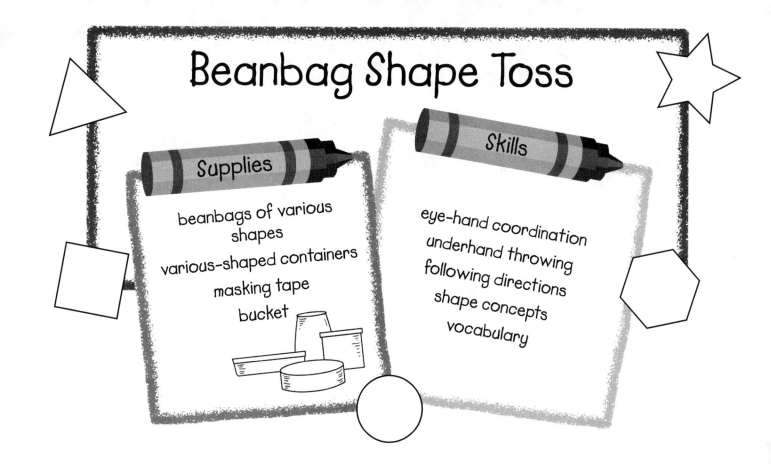

Supplies

beanbags of various shapes

various-shaped containers

masking tape

bucket

Skills

eye-hand coordination

underhand throwing

following directions

shape concepts

vocabulary

Instructions for Teacher

1. Arrange containers (round, square, rectangular, triangular) in a row on the floor.
2. Place a tape line on the floor four to six feet away for children to stand behind during the activity. Place various-shaped beanbags in a bucket in front of the line.
3. Demonstrate throwing the beanbags underhand into a container.
4. Have the children name the beanbag shapes and shapes of the containers they are thrown into.

Instructions for Child

1. Pick up a shape beanbag and throw it underhand into the shape container. (Example: "Pick up a square beanbag and throw it into the round basket.")
2. Tell the teacher what you did. ("I threw the square beanbag into the round basket.")

Gross Motor Shapes

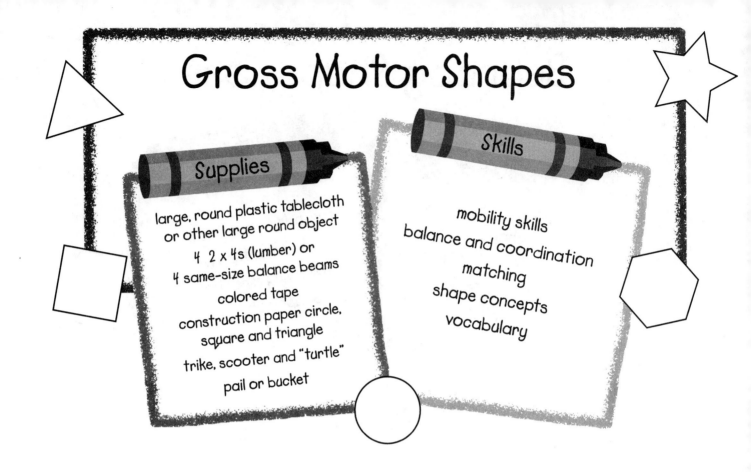

Supplies

large, round plastic tablecloth or other large round object

4 2 x 4s (lumber) or 4 same-size balance beams

colored tape

construction paper circle, square and triangle

trike, scooter and "turtle"

pail or bucket

Skills

mobility skills
balance and coordination
matching
shape concepts
vocabulary

Instructions for Teacher

1. Place a large plastic tablecloth or other large round object (Example: A plastic swimming pool) on the floor. If using a tablecloth, secure firmly to the floor.
2. Several feet away, arrange the 2 x 4s or balance beams on the floor so they form a square. Secure them so they don't slip as children walk on them.
3. Using colored tape, make a large triangle on the floor several feet away from the other shapes.
4. Place construction paper shapes in a pail or bucket.

Instructions for Child

1. Reach into the pail and pull out a paper shape.
2. Name the shape. Listen to the teacher's instructions. (Examples: "Ride the scooter around the circle" or "Walk, keeping your balance on the square.")
3. Follow the instructions.

Variations

Add to the complexity of the directions by telling the child how many times to do the task.

Fall

TLC10470 Copyright © Teaching & Learning Company, Carthage, IL 62321-0010

Pinecone Drop

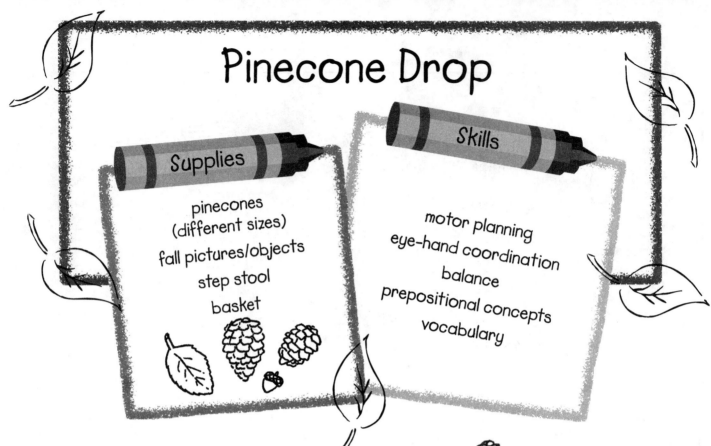

Supplies

pinecones
(different sizes)
fall pictures/objects
step stool
basket

Skills

motor planning
eye-hand coordination
balance
prepositional concepts
vocabulary

Instructions for Teacher

1. Place various-sized pinecones in a basket next to a step stool. On the floor in front of the step stool, arrange fall pictures and/or objects.
2. Demonstrate the pinecone drop: pick up one pinecone, climb the step stool, extend an arm out and drop the pinecone on a specific picture/object. Name the picture/object.

Instructions for Child

1. Pick up a pinecone and tell if it is big or small.
2. Climb the step stool (with teacher help if needed). Drop the pinecone over the pictures/objects.
3. Name the picture/object the pinecone landed on or near.

Variations

Encourage the child to describe the picture/object the pinecone landed on or near. Use fall objects other than pinecones.

Acorn Walk

Supplies

acorns (different sizes)
spoons (big/small)
traffic cones

Skills

eye-hand coordination
grasp and prehension
motor planning
balance
size concepts
vocabulary

Instructions for Teacher

1. Set a starting point. Then place a cone approximately 10 feet away.
2. Place a container of acorns and spoons at the starting point.
3. Demonstrate how to place an acorn on a spoon, and balance it while you walk around the cone and return to start.

Instructions for Child

1. Take a spoon and an acorn.
2. Tell the teacher the size of the spoon and acorn (big or small).
3. Stand on the starting point and put the acorn on the spoon (with teacher help if needed).
4. On the signal "go," walk around the cone and return to the starting point without dropping the acorn from the spoon.

Variations

Time the activity, change the direction (sideways or backwards) or rate (fast or slow) of the walk. Change the acorn to different autumn objects. Pair up students or create teams.

Finding Fall

Supplies

child's plastic swimming pool or sand table

leaves (clean and dry)

fall objects (acorns, pinecones, etc.)

blindfold

Skills

sensory: touch, smell

tactile discrimination

vocabulary

Instructions for Teacher

1. Place a swimming pool/sand table on the floor.
2. Show fall objects to the children, allowing them to name and touch the objects.
3. Put objects in the pool and cover them with clean, dry leaves.
4. Demonstrate how to feel for the hidden objects while blindfolded.

Instructions for Child

1. Go to the table when your name is called to be blindfolded by the teacher.
2. Move your hands through the leaves in search of a fall object. When you find one, try to guess what it is by feeling it.
3. Take off the blindfold to see if your guess was correct!

Variations

Use packing peanuts instead of leaves for a winter "snow" theme.

Pin the Tail on the Squirrel

Supplies

template—large squirrel
and tail, page 40
fuzzy material
blindfold
masking tape

Skills

aiming
body and spatial awareness
tactile exploration
visual memory
prepositional concepts
vocabulary

Instructions for Teacher

1. Enlarge the squirrel template and cut it out.
2. Enlarge the squirrel tail and cut it out. Glue fuzzy material on it. Stick rolled-up masking tape on the back of the tail.
3. Tape the squirrel to a wall at an appropriate height for a child to reach.
4. Place a tape line on the floor five to six feet away from the squirrel.
5. Demonstrate how to "pin the tail on the squirrel" while blindfolded.

Instructions for Child

1. Stand behind the tape line.
2. Hold the squirrel's tail.
3. Wait to be blindfolded. Turn around once and walk slowly toward the squirrel. Attach the tail where you think it goes.
4. Remove the blindfold to see the where you put the tail. Name where the tail landed (above/below, on/off or next to/close to) the squirrel.

Large Squirrel and Tail

Seasons

Dress the Scarecrow

Supplies

template-scarecrow cut from cardstock (one for each child), page 42

template-scarecrow clothing, page 43

different textured materials (fabric, felt, burlap, straw)

glue

Skills

pasting
visual discrimination
tactile exploration
body parts
following directions
vocabulary

Instructions for Teacher

1. Cut out a scarecrow and clothing items for each child. Glue the textured materials on the clothing items. Leave the straw loose. Prepare a model to show the children.
2. Give each child a pre-cut scarecrow. Place the clothing items on the table.
3. Name the clothing items and say where each belongs on the scarecrow's body. Show the children the completed model.
4. Give verbal instructions, allowing children to fill in the last word:
   A. Pick up the hat and glue it on his _____.
   B. Pick up the coat and glue it on his _____.
   C. Pick up the boots and glue them on his _____.
   D. Pick up the gloves and glue them on his _____.
   E. Pick up the straw and glue it on his _____ and _____.

Instructions for Child

1. Choose a hat, coat, boots, gloves and straw for the scarecrow.
2. Follow the teacher's directions.
3. Talk about the scarecrow with a friend.

Variations

Have the child cut out the clothing and glue the textured materials on it.

Scarecrow

Scarecrow Clothing

Seasons

Winter

TLC10470 Copyright © Teaching & Learning Company, Carthage, IL 62321-0010

Ice Cube Race

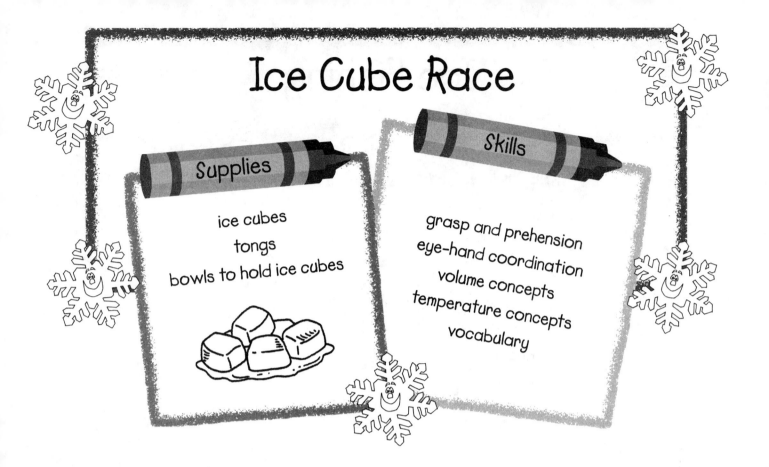

Supplies

ice cubes
tongs
bowls to hold ice cubes

Skills

grasp and prehension
eye-hand coordination
volume concepts
temperature concepts
vocabulary

Instructions for Teacher

1. Place a number of ice cubes in a bowl with a set of tongs and an empty dish beside it.
2. Demonstrate to the children how the tongs open and close when squeezed together by an index finger and thumb.
3. Demonstrate how to use the tongs to pick up an ice cube and place it in the dish.

Instructions for Child

1. Practice squeezing the tongs.
2. Pick up an ice cube using only the tongs and put it in the empty dish. Continue moving the ice cubes one at a time until the bowl is empty and the dish is full.

Variations

Race against each other or against the clock.

Ice Fishing

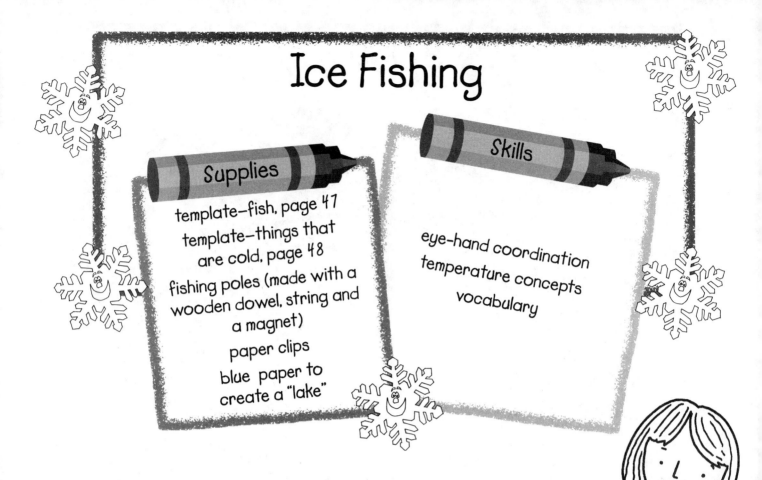

Supplies

template–fish, page 47

template–things that are cold, page 48

fishing poles (made with a wooden dowel, string and a magnet)

paper clips

blue paper to create a "lake"

Skills

eye-hand coordination

temperature concepts

vocabulary

Instructions for Teacher

1. Make three copies of the fish template and cut them out.
2. Cut out the pictures of things that are cold on the template and glue one on each fish.
3. Attach a paper clip to the mouth of each fish.
4. Lay the fish on a "lake" of blue paper on the floor. Put the fishing poles beside the lake.
5. Demonstrate the proper way to hold the fishing pole with two hands. Show how to maneuver the pole so the magnet hooks itself to the paper clip on a fish and can be picked up.

Instructions for Child

1. Pick up the fishing pole with two hands and stand by the lake. Lower the fishing pole into the lake, catch a fish, then remove it from the "hook."
2. Name the cold item you caught.

Variations

Use items that pertain to cold. Use fish that have pictures relating to other themes: numbers, shapes, animals, etc.

Fish

Things That Are Cold

Seasons

Ice Skating

Supplies

2 one-foot squares of felt per child

objects for obstacle course

Skills

balance and coordination
motor planning
prepositional concepts
vocabulary

Instructions for Teacher

1. Design an obstacle course on the floor using any variety of items for the child to "skate" around (around a cone, between two stuffed animals, under a basketball hoop, beside a snowman, etc.).

2. Demonstrate "felt skating" to the child. Put two felt squares on the floor. Put one foot on each square. Begin sliding your feet along the floor on the felt pieces. Emphasize keeping your feet on the floor so the felt "skates" don't fall off.

Instructions for Child

1. Practice skating by sliding your feet over the floor on felt squares.

2. "Skate" around the obstacle course. Talk about the objects you are skating next to, around, between, in front of, in back of, etc.

Variations

Skate with a partner.

Note: This activity works best on wood or tile floors. If the floor is carpeted, substitute wax paper for the felt.

Mitten Match

Supplies

template-mittens
(several pairs), page 51
wallpaper samples
clip clothespins
clothesline

Skills

grasp and prehension
bilateral skills
eye-hand coordination
matching
prepositional concept
vocabulary

Instructions for Teacher

1. Cut 10 pairs of mittens out of different designs of wallpaper, using the mitten template.
2. Create two piles of mittens with each pile containing one mitten from each pair.
3. Hang the clothesline low enough for children to reach.
4. Demonstrate how to open and close the clothespins using only an index finger and thumb.

Instructions for Child

1. Practice opening and closing clothespins.
2. Pick a mitten from one pile. Go to the second pile and find its match.
3. Clip the matched mittens on the clothesline using a clothespin.

Variations

Use real children's mittens.

Note: If time permits, practice taking the pair of mittens on and off the clothesline.

Mittens

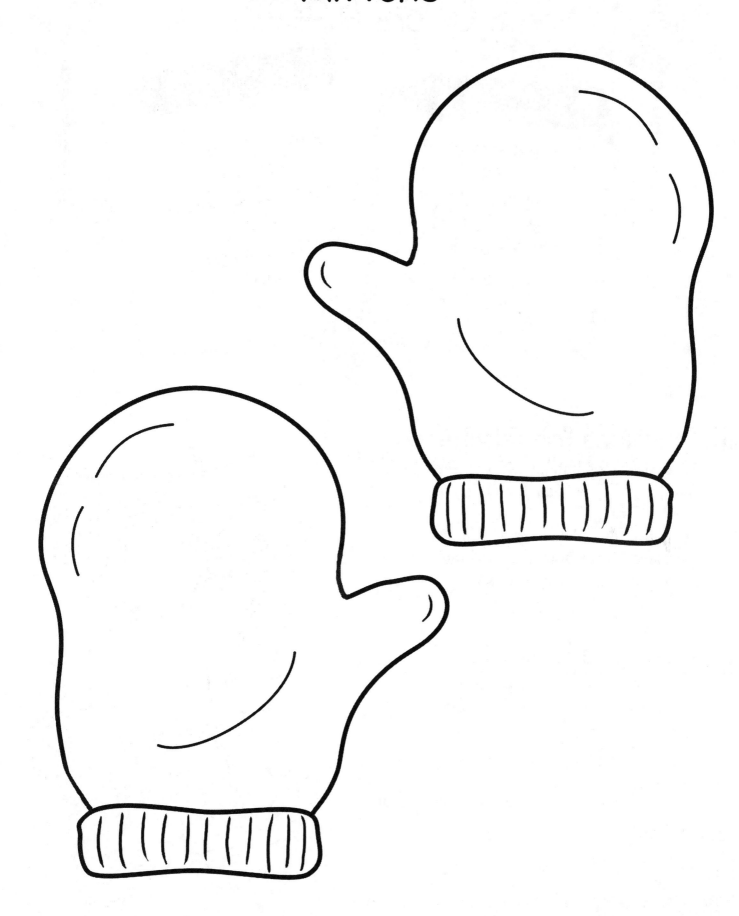

Wheelbarrow Walk over "Crunchy Snow"

Supplies

sheets of bubble wrap
tape

Skills

strength
sensory: touch and proprioception
balancing
vocabulary

Instructions for Teacher

1. Tape sheets of bubble wrap securely to the floor, creating a road for children to travel over.
2. Demonstrate a wheelbarrow walk, walking on the hands with someone holding the feet. Decide if a teacher or peer should hold each child's feet.

Instructions for Child

Walk on your hands over a sheet of bubble wrap, listening to the "crunchy snow" as the bubbles pop along the road.

Variations

Crawl, ride a scooter or logroll over the bubble wrap.

Spring

April Showers

Supplies

child-safe umbrella
balance beam

Skills

balance and coordination
motor planning
following directions
prepositional concepts
vocabulary

Instructions for Teacher

Set up the balance beam and place the closed umbrella at one end.

Instructions for Child

1. Pick up the umbrella.
2. Walk back and forth across the balance beam holding the closed umbrella.
3. Open up the umbrella and hold it above your head, walking back and forth across the balance beam.

Variations

Walk backwards, sideways, in small steps or large steps. Have the child follow directions, such as: "Walk down the beam with the umbrella open and at your side." "Walk back with the umbrella closed, holding it above your head."

TLC10470 Copyright © Teaching & Learning Company, Carthage, IL 62321-0010

May Flowers

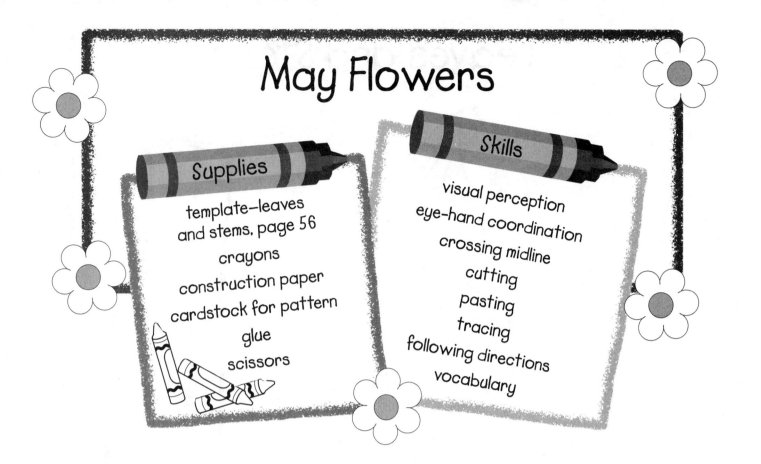

Supplies

template—leaves
and stems, page 56

crayons

construction paper

cardstock for pattern

glue

scissors

Skills

visual perception

eye-hand coordination

crossing midline

cutting

pasting

tracing

following directions

vocabulary

Instructions for Teacher

1. Cut patterns for leaves and a stem out of cardstock using the template.
2. Place all other supplies on a table.
3. Demonstrate the skill of tracing the stem, leaves and your hand.
4. Prepare a visual example of this project for the child to follow.

Instructions for Child

1. Lay one hand on a sheet of colored construction paper. With a crayon, carefully trace around your hand without moving it. Lift your hand off the paper and see a beautiful flower!
2. Cut out the flower.
3. Trace the two leaf patterns and one stem pattern on green construction paper.
4. Cut out the leaves and stem.
5. Glue all parts of the flower onto a piece of construction paper using the teacher's project as a guide.

Variations

Make a colorful bouquet of flowers or have everyone in the class make a flower for a classroom bulletin board.

Leaves and Stems

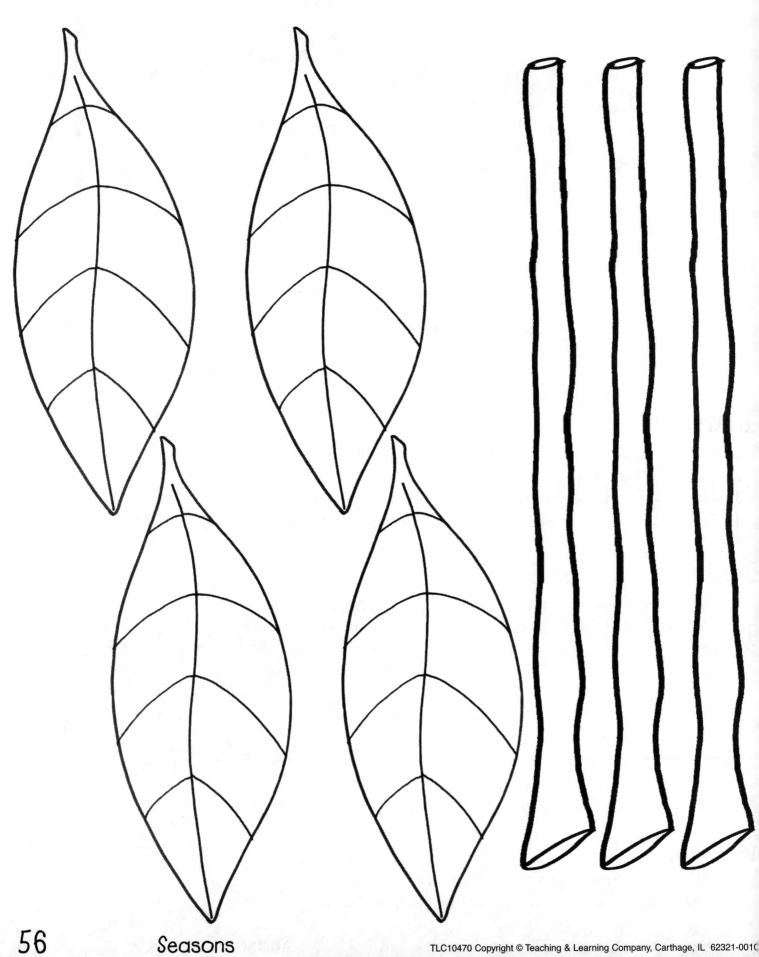

Seasons

Fill the Bird Feeder

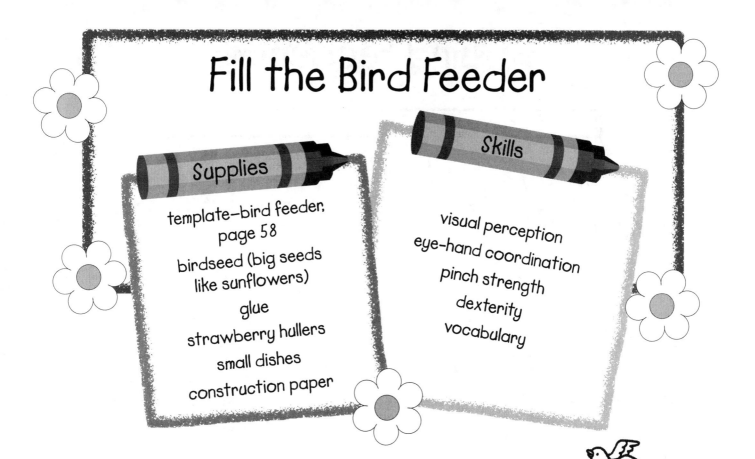

Supplies

template–bird feeder, page 58

birdseed (big seeds like sunflowers)

glue

strawberry hullers

small dishes

construction paper

Skills

visual perception

eye-hand coordination

pinch strength

dexterity

vocabulary

Instructions for Teacher

1. Make a copy of the bird feeder template for each child and one for a model.
2. Place birdseed in small dishes on the table with glue and strawberry hullers.
3. Demonstrating how to hold the strawberry huller using an index finger and thumb, pick up birdseed and place it on the feeder.

Instructions for Child

1. Put dots of glue on the bird feeder.
2. Use the strawberry huller to pick up a seed, then put it on a drop of glue.
3. Continue until every drop of glue has a seed on it.

Bird Feeder

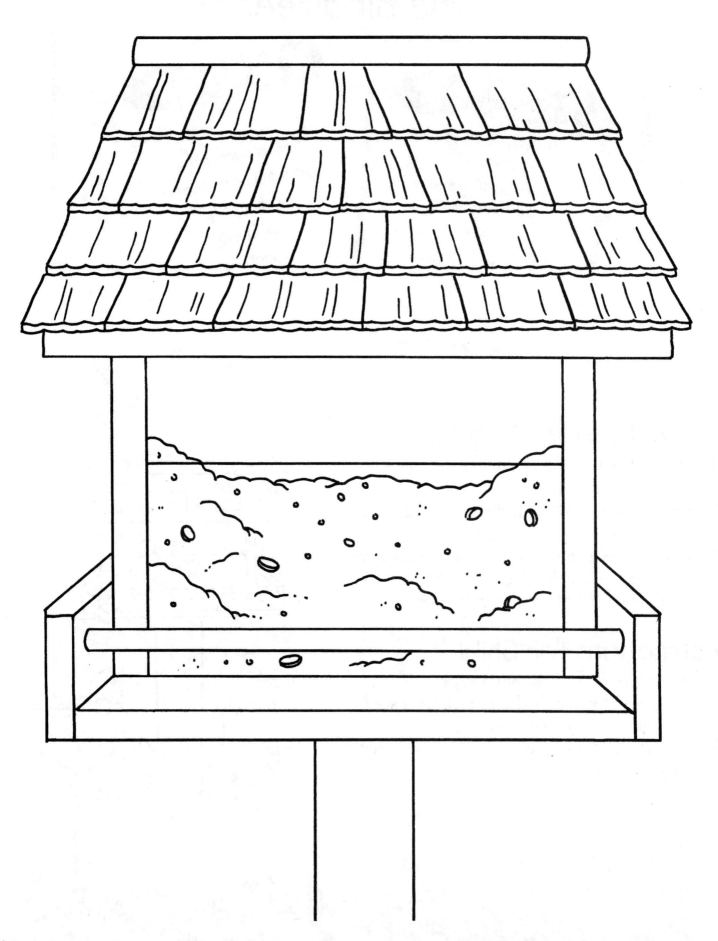

Seasons

Go Fly a Kite

Supplies

diamond-shape pattern for kite

spring pictures cut from magazines

stapler

crepe paper streamers

markers

glue

supplies for kite decoration

Skills

visual perception

eye-hand coordination

strength

dexterity

vocabulary

Instructions for Teacher

1. Draw a diamond shape kite pattern and copy it for each child.
2. Cut spring pictures (flowers, birds, etc.) from magazines.
3. Cut crepe paper streamers into two-foot lengths.
4. Give each child a copy of the kite, some spring pictures and one crepe paper streamer.

Instructions for Child

1. Cut out the kite and decorate it.
2. Staple the long crepe paper tail onto the bottom of the kite.
3. Staple or glue the spring pictures onto the kite.
4. Talk with a friend about the kite and the spring pictures.

Variations

Use thematic pictures or use different textures for the tail of the kite.

A Tisket, a Tasket

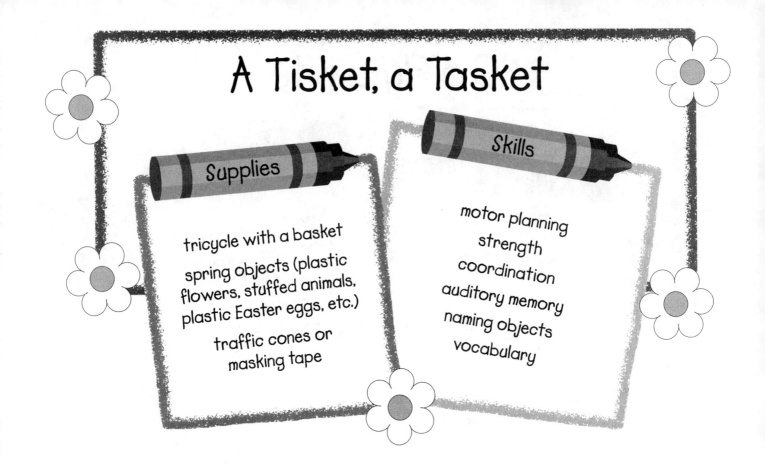

Supplies

tricycle with a basket

spring objects (plastic flowers, stuffed animals, plastic Easter eggs, etc.)

traffic cones or masking tape

Skills

motor planning
strength
coordination
auditory memory
naming objects
vocabulary

Instructions for Teacher

1. Set up a curvy tricycle path using cones or masking tape and place spring objects along the path. Set a starting point at the beginning of the course.

Instructions for Child

1. Get on the tricycle at the starting point.
2. Listen carefully for directions from the teacher to pick up and place three different objects in the basket along the path. (Example: "Pick up the yellow egg, the red flower and the baby bunny.")
3. Pedal down the path looking for the objects. When you find one, get off the tricycle and pick it up.
4. Place it in the basket and get back on the tricycle.
5. Find all three objects and put them in the basket.
6. Hold up each of the objects in the basket and name it when you get back to your starting place.

Variations

Time the activity or change the number of objects to be remembered.

Halloween

Ghost Windsock

Supplies

template-ghosts, page 63
white crepe paper
streamers
white or black yarn
glue sticks
stapler
scissors
hole punch

Skills

visual perceptual motor
grasp and prehension
dexterity
pasting
body parts
vocabulary

Instructions for Teacher

1. Make a copy of the template for each child and one for a model.
2. Cut crepe paper streamers into strips about $^3/_4$" x 10".
3. Cut along the line on the template to separate the two ghosts.
4. Assemble the model by gluing crepe paper strips on the inside of the body.
5. Roll the body into a cylinder and staple it, overlapping approximately one inch. Punch holes on opposite sides of the top of the windsock and run the yarn through to make a hanger.
6. Give each child a ghost body and eight or nine crepe paper strips.

Instructions for Child

1. Look at the ghost windsock and make one that looks like it.
2. Turn the ghost body over and glue the crepe paper strips on it.
3. The teacher will help you staple the ends of your windsock together.
4. Tie a yarn handle in the holes.

Ghosts

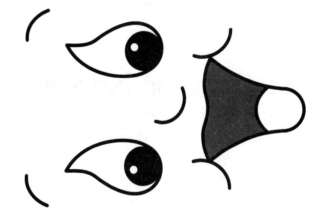

Pumpkin Whackers

Supplies

newspapers
masking tape
orange balloons
net

Skills

eye-hand coordination
motor planning
visual tracking
strength
vocabulary

Instructions for Teacher

1. Make whackers out of rolled up newspapers held together with masking tape.
2. Blow up orange balloons.
3. Set up a net to divide the space into an area for two teams.
4. Divide the children into two teams and have each team stand on opposite sides of the net.
5. Demonstrate how to "whack" the balloon over the net.
6. Provide each child with a balloon and whacker.
7. Encourage them to hit the balloons back and forth over the net (but not to hit each other).

Instructions for Child

1. Hit the "pumpkin" balloon over the net. When someone hits one to you, hit it back.
2. Try to keep it up in the air as long as you can.

Variations

Give each child a balloon and a whacker. Have them hit their balloons repeatedly into the air.

Pumpkin Bowling

Supplies

6 plastic bowling pins

6 circles of white fabric (large enough to cover the bowling pins)

12 small black pom-poms (approximately $\frac{1}{2}$")

6 black pipe cleaners

glue

small pumpkin (for a bowling ball)

Skills

eye-hand coordination

strength

counting

number concepts

vocabulary

Instructions for Teacher

1. Make fabric ghosts to cover the bowling pins: Glue two small pom-poms on them for eyes. Drape the fabric over each bowling pin and secure it at the "neck" with a pipe cleaner.
2. Set up the ghost pins. Place a spot on the floor six to eight feet away for the child to stand. Remove the stem from the pumpkin.
3. Demonstrate how to squat down and roll the pumpkin along the floor to knock down the ghost pins. Tell the child not to throw or bounce the pumpkin, but just roll it along the floor!

Instructions for Child

1. Stand on the spot and pick up the pumpkin.
2. Squat down and roll the pumpkin on the floor to knock over the ghosts.
3. Count the number of ghosts you knock down. Tell how many are left standing.
4. Keep trying until you knock the last ghost pin down.

Variations

Use an orange ball instead of a pumpkin.

Candy Corn Shakers

Supplies

empty baby food jars
candy corn
tongs
Halloween stickers

Skills

grasp and prehension
dexterity
eye-hand coordination
vocabulary

Instructions for Teacher

1. Clean and remove labels from enough baby food jars for each child and one model.
2. Make a candy corn shaker model by filling one of the jars about $2/3$ full of candy corn. Replace the lid, and decorate the jar with Halloween stickers.
3. Demonstrate how to use the tongs to pick up a piece of candy corn and put it in a jar.
4. Give each child a baby food jar, some candy corn, a pair of tongs and Halloween stickers.

Instructions for Child

1. Look at the candy corn shaker model.
2. Use the tongs, with your thumb and index finger, to pick up candy corn and put it in your jar. Don't fill the jar, but put in enough to look like the model.
3. Screw on the lid and decorate the jar with stickers.
4. Shake the shaker to make a loud noise.

Pumpkin Pull

Supplies

various-sized pumpkins
and gourds

traffic cones
and obstacles

wagon

Skills

strength
coordination
weight concepts
texture concepts
prepositional concepts
vocabulary

Instructions for Teacher

1. Set up an obstacle course of traffic cones or other objects.
2. Place an empty wagon next to several pumpkins and gourds of various sizes and shapes at the beginning of the obstacle course.
3. Demonstrate how to fill the wagon with pumpkins and gourds, and go through the obstacle course.
4. Emphasize the concepts of light/heavy, big/small, bumpy/ smooth, etc.

Instructions for Child

1. Fill the wagon with pumpkins and gourds,
2. Pull the wagon through the obstacle course, following the teacher's directions.
3. Tell the teacher what you are doing as you go through the obstacle course.
4. When you get back to the starting place, unload the wagon.

Variations

Counting can easily be incorporated into this activity.

Thanksgiving

Cranberry Float

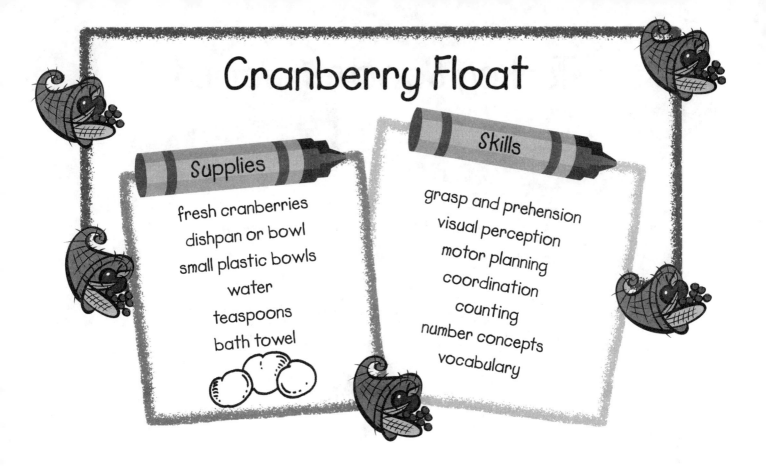

Supplies

fresh cranberries
dishpan or bowl
small plastic bowls
water
teaspoons
bath towel

Skills

grasp and prehension
visual perception
motor planning
coordination
counting
number concepts
vocabulary

Instructions for Teacher

1. Fill a dishpan half full of water and put approximately 30 cranberries in the water. Place a bowl beside the dishpan. (Put a bath towel underneath the dishpan to absorb any water that spills out.)
2. Place teaspoons by the dishpan.

Instructions for Child

1. Pick up a teaspoon, put it in the water, and scoop up a cranberry. (The child may need assistance to grasp and hold the spoon to prevent the cranberry from falling off.)
2. Carefully dump the cranberry into the bowl without dropping it.
3. Continue until you have 10 cranberries in the bowl.
4. Count aloud the number of your cranberries. Do you have 10?

Variations

Time the activity.

Turkey Scooter Scoot

Supplies

scooter boards

fall objects (small pumpkin, acorn, pinecone, apple, leaves, etc.)

3 plastic bowls or shoe boxes

Skills

strength

coordination

motor planning

prepositional concepts

vocabulary

Instructions for Teacher

1. Set up three stations along a 20-foot scooter board path. Each station will contain a variety of fall objects and a plastic bowl.

2. As the child moves from station to station, the teacher will provide specific directions at each one using the selected objects and a variety of prepositions ("Put the pumpkin under the bowl." "Put the leaf on the side of the bowl.").

Instructions for Child

1. Lie tummy-down on the scooter board and push yourself down the path to the first station. Wait at the first station for instructions from the teacher.

2. Follow the instructions given by the teacher, then tell the teacher what you did ("I put the pumpkin under the bowl.").

3. Push yourself on the scooter board to the second station and wait for more instructions from the teacher.

4. Continue to the third station and do what the teacher tells you.

Thanksgiving Table

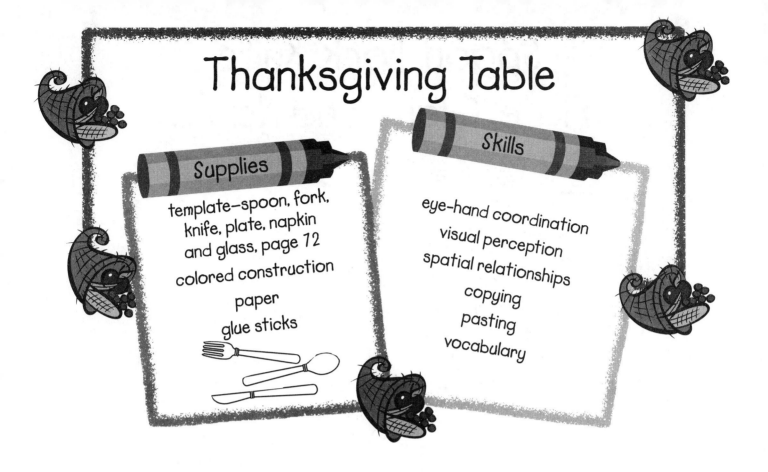

Supplies

template—spoon, fork, knife, plate, napkin and glass, page 72

colored construction paper

glue sticks

Skills

eye-hand coordination

visual perception

spatial relationships

copying

pasting

vocabulary

Instructions for Teacher

1. Using the template patterns, cut out a spoon, fork, knife, plate, napkin and glass for each child. Lay them on a table.
2. Assemble one table setting on a construction paper place mat to use as a model.
3. Ask questions: "What utensil is that?" "What kind of food do you eat with a spoon?" "What kind of Thanksgiving food do you have to cut with a knife?"

Instructions for Child

1. Take a piece of construction paper for your place mat.
2. Get a spoon, fork, knife, plate, napkin and glass.
3. Copying the teacher's model, glue your pieces onto the place mat.
4. Answer the teacher's questions.

Variations

Use letters, colors, shapes and pictures instead of numbers.

Spoon, Fork, Knife, Plate, Glass and Napkin

Holidays

Fruity Fun with Friends

Supplies

1 wooden kabob stick
for every child

paper plates

soft fruit cut
in small pieces

Skills

dexterity

sensory: taste

sequencing

vocabulary

Instructions for Teacher

1. Put different kinds of fruit in separate bowls with a spoon for each on a table.
2. At one end of the table place paper plates and kabob sticks.
3. Prepare a fruit kabob as a model for the children.

Instructions for Child

1. Go to the table and pick up a paper plate and a kabob stick.
2. Stop at each fruit bowl, take one piece of fruit with the spoon, and put it on your plate.
3. Look at the kabob your teacher made. Put the fruit on your kabob stick to make it look like the model.

Safety Tip

Cut off the pointed tip of the bamboo skewers with snippers.

Corn Relay

Supplies

dried corn or candied corn

tablespoon for each child

2 bowls

Skills

eye-hand coordination

dexterity

turn-taking

teamwork

vocabulary

Instructions for Teacher

1. Divide the children into two groups and have them line up side by side. The lines should be facing each other several feet apart.
2. Put the corn in two bowls on the floor beside the first children in the lines. Give each child a tablespoon.
3. Demonstrate how to take a spoonful of corn and empty it into the spoon of the child standing next in line.

Instructions for Child

1. When the teacher says "go," reach down and pick up some corn with your spoon.
2. Carefully pour the corn into the spoon of the person standing next to you.
3. Continue until the corn is in the last person's spoon.
4. The last person walks to the front of the line and drops the corn back into the bowl.
5. Then the first person in the line goes to the end and the next person picks up a spoonful of corn.
6. Continue until everyone has had a turn at being first and last.

Christmas

Pulling Santa's Toy Bag

Supplies

large pillowcase

traffic cones or Christmas items to create an obstacle course

Skills

strength

motor planning

following directions

weight concepts

vocabulary

Instructions for Teacher

1. Fill a large pillowcase $1/2$ to $3/4$ full of books until it is the desired weight. The weight of the bag can be adjusted according to the strength of the child. Tell the children this is Santa's bag.
2. Create a circular obstacle course with the same starting and ending point on the floor using cones, Christmas items and packages. Space the items far enough apart so the bag can be pulled through them.

Instructions for Child

1. Gather the end of the pillowcase and hold it with one or two hands.
2. Drag or carry it through the obstacle course, being careful not to let it touch any items along the way.
3. Name the Christmas items as you drag the bag past them.

Variations

Fill the sack with toys and drop them off at stations along the obstacle course. Start with an empty sack and pick up objects along the obstacle course to fill Santa's bag.

Fishing for Toys

Supplies

templates—fish, page 78

fishing pole (made with wooden dowel, string, and magnet)

6 large paper clips

large piece of blue paper, tablecloth or sheet (for water)

Skills

eye-hand coordination
following directions
vocabulary

Instructions for Teacher

1. Cut out the six fish from the template.
2. Attach a paper clip to each fish's mouth.
3. Assemble the fishing poles.
4. Place the "water" on the floor and arrange the fish on it.
5. Demonstrate how to hold the fishing pole with both hands, maneuvering it so the magnet attaches to a paper clip on a fish.

Instructions for Child

1. Pick up a fishing pole and stand by the water.
2. Lower the line into the water and "hook" a fish.
3. Pull the fish from the water. Take it off the "hook" and name the toy on the fish.

Variations

Ask questions related to each toy; have the child fish for a specific toy; have the child fish for a toy described by the teacher ("Fish for a toy that has wheels").

Fish

Holidays

Light Up the Tree

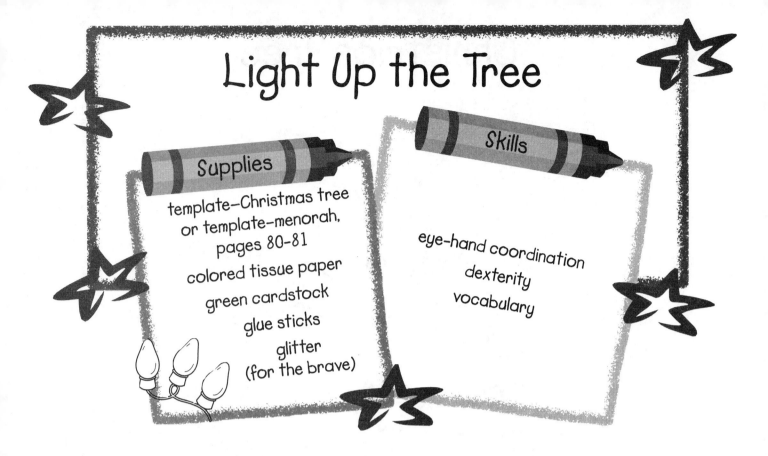

Supplies

template—Christmas tree
or template-menorah,
pages 80-81
colored tissue paper
green cardstock
glue sticks
glitter
(for the brave)

Skills

eye-hand coordination
dexterity
vocabulary

Instructions for Teacher

1. Cut a Christmas tree out of green cardstock for each child. Cut colored tissue paper into two-inch squares.
2. Make a model Christmas tree with tissue paper balls on it to show the children.
3. Give each child a Christmas tree, several tissue paper squares, a glue stick and some glitter (optional).
4. Demonstrate how to use the thumb and fingertips to roll the paper into a ball.

Instructions for Child

1. Pick up your tissue squares and roll them into balls.
2. Glue the balls onto the tree to "light it up."

Variations

Give each child a copy of the tree template and have them color it green before gluing on the tissue paper balls.

Encourage the children to talk about decorations they put on their tree at home.

Light the Menorah: Use the menorah template and have children

Christmas Tree

Menorah

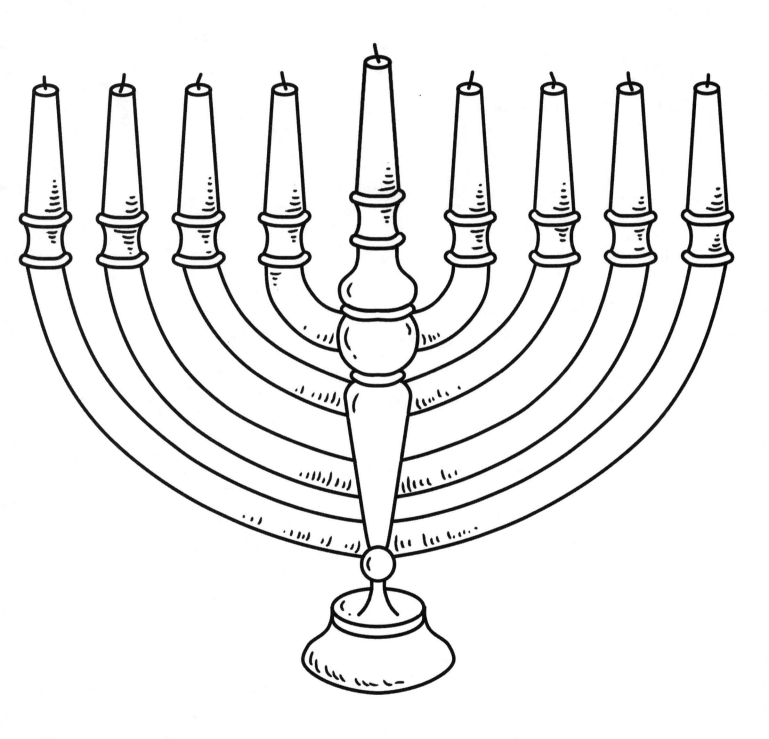

Holiday Greeting Card Collage

Supplies

fronts of recycled
holiday greeting cards

scissors

glue

large paper tree
cut from butcher paper

Skills

eye-hand coordination

dexterity

cutting

pasting

vocabulary

Instructions for Teacher

1. Cut out a large tree from butcher paper to use as the foundation for the collage.
2. Using a marker, draw a circle on each holiday card picture to indicate what the child should cut out.
3. Spread the cards on a table.
4. When the collage is completed, hang it on the wall and talk with the children about it. (Ask "How many snowmen do you see?" "Can you find three animals?" etc.)

Instructions for Child

1. Pick a card and cut out the picture, following the line marked by the teacher.
2. Take your picture to the tree and glue it on. Make sure it is not touching another picture.
3. Answer the teacher's questions.

82   Holidays

Holiday Listening

Supplies

holiday die-cuts

colored construction paper

3 10" diameter construction paper circles (red, green, blue)

Skills

following directions
auditory memory
vocabulary

Instructions for Teacher

1. Prepare several die-cuts of holiday items using a different color of paper for each, (red for Santas, green for trees).
2. Arrange a few colored markers (such as construction paper circles) on the floor and spread out the die-cuts.
3. Give instructions to each child based on his or her skills.

Instructions for Child

1. Listen and follow my directions:

Complex Directions: "Pick up three red Santas and two green trees and put them on the red circle."

Simple Directions: "Pick up two yellow angels and give them to me."

Valentine's Day

TLC10470 Copyright © Teaching & Learning Company, Carthage, IL 62321-0010

Lacing Valentines

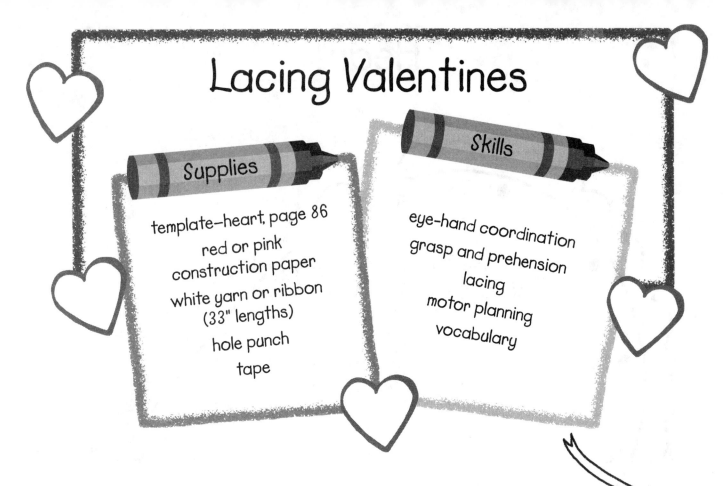

Supplies

template–heart, page 86

red or pink construction paper

white yarn or ribbon (33" lengths)

hole punch

tape

Skills

eye-hand coordination

grasp and prehension

lacing

motor planning

vocabulary

Instructions for Teacher

1. Using the template pattern, cut out a construction paper heart for each child and one to use as a sample.
2. Punch holes around the perimeter of the hearts at one-inch intervals.
3. Cut the yarn or ribbon in 33-inch lengths. Cover one end with tape for easy lacing.
4. Prepare the sample heart by lacing the yarn or ribbon in and out of the holes. When all the holes have been laced, tie the ends in a bow at the top.
5. Have the children sit at a table. Give each of them a heart and a yarn or ribbon lace. Show them how to push the taped end of the lace through the holes. Tape the end of the yarn at the back of the heart to keep it from slipping back through.

Instructions for Child

1. Lace your heart by weaving the yarn (or ribbon) in the first hole.
2. Tape the end of the yarn on the back of the heart. Then continue lacing.
3. When you are done lacing, ask the teacher to help tie a bow.

Heart

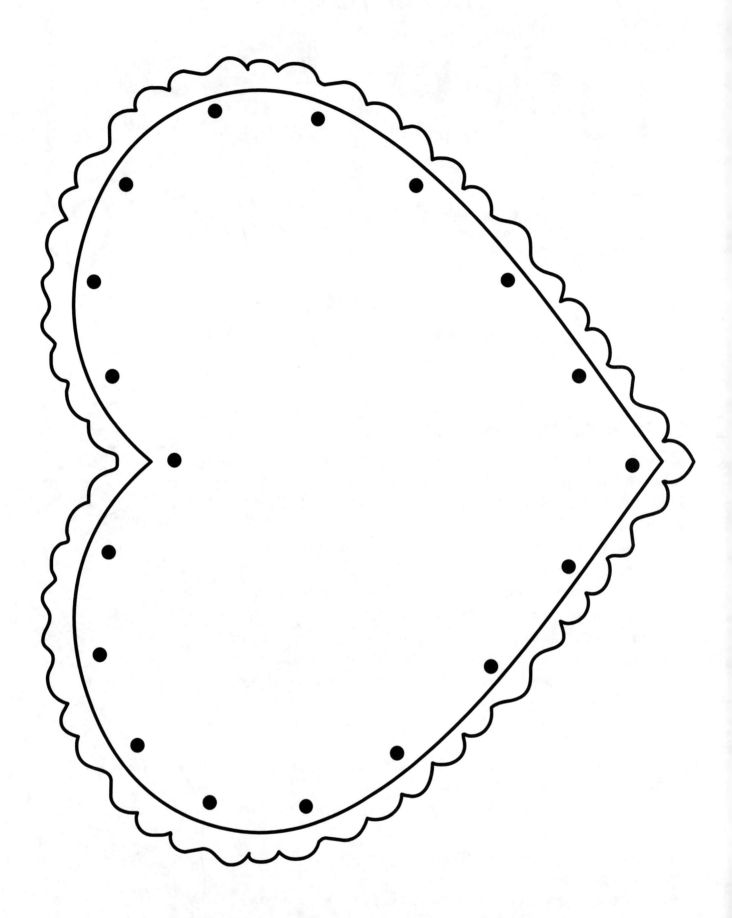

Holidays

Special Delivery

Supplies

valentines
pail or bucket
cardboard box
traffic cones
scooter or tricycle
colored tape or
colored spot

Skills

strength and agility
balance and coordination
motor planning
following directions
counting
vocabulary

Instructions for Teacher

1. Place the valentines in the pail or bucket. Make a "mailbox" out of a cardboard box.
2. Mark a starting point on the floor with a tape line or colored spot. Place the mailbox approximately 30 feet away.
3. Put the scooter or tricycle and the pail of valentines at the starting place.
4. Arrange traffic cones at intervals several feet apart between the starting place and the mailbox.
5. Demonstrate how to weave in and out of the traffic cones to get to the mailbox and back to the starting place.

Instructions for Child

1. Take X number of valentines out of the pail. Count out loud as you do this.
2. Ride the scooter or tricycle to the mailbox by going in and out of the traffic cones.
3. Mail the valentines and ride back to start by going in and out of the cones.

Valentine Tiddly Winks

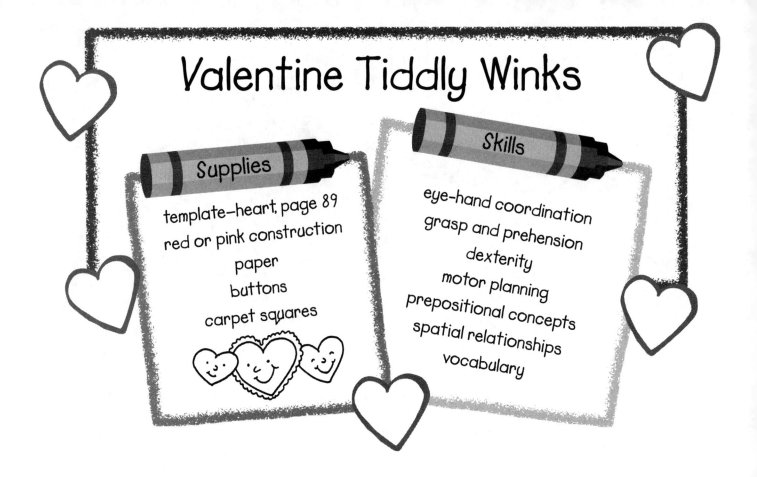

Supplies

template–heart, page 89
red or pink construction paper
buttons
carpet squares

Skills

eye-hand coordination
grasp and prehension
dexterity
motor planning
prepositional concepts
spatial relationships
vocabulary

Instructions for Teacher

1. Using the template, cut out hearts to use as targets for the game.
2. Line up carpet squares on the floor for children to sit on. Place a heart on the floor in front of each carpet square.
3. Demonstrate how to hold a button between the thumb and index finger and use it to snap another button onto the heart target.
4. Give each child at least two buttons.

Instructions for Child

1. Kneel on your carpet square.
2. Hold one button as the teacher did and try to snap another button onto the heart target.
3. Tell the teacher where your button landed (on, off, behind, next to, near the heart, etc.).

Heart

Sweetheart Mice

Supplies

template—mouse, page 91

white, red and pink construction paper

glue sticks

black pipe cleaners

Skills

visual perception

copying

pasting

size concepts

body parts

vocabulary

Instructions for Teacher

1. Cut out the large heart (face), two medium hearts (ears) and three small hearts (eyes and nose) from construction paper using the template for each mouse.
2. Snip pipe cleaners into three-inch lengths (whiskers). You will need six for each mouse.
3. Assemble a model for the children to copy.
4. Give each child one large heart, two medium hearts, three small hearts, six three-inch pipe cleaners and a glue stick.
5. Emphasize size concepts (small, medium, large, biggest, smallest and tiny).

Instructions for Child

1. Look at the mouse model. Make a mouse like it.
2. Use the biggest heart for the face, the medium-sized hearts for the ears and the small hearts for the eyes and nose.
3. Glue the hearts together to make the mouse's face like the model.
4. Glue the pipe cleaner whiskers on your mouse.

Mouse

Holidays

Rosy Applesauce Slurp

Supplies

pink applesauce
cinnamon
small cups
stirrers
drinking straws

Skills

oral motor
tasting
vocabulary

Instructions for Teacher

1. Put some applesauce in a small cup for each child.
2. Cut straws into four-inch lengths.
3. Have the children sit at a table and give each one a cup of applesauce, a stirrer and a straw.
4. Demonstrate how to mix a little cinnamon into the applesauce using a stirrer.
5. Let each child smell the cinnamon, then help them sprinkle a little on their applesauce.

Instructions for Child

1. Stir the cinnamon into your applesauce.
2. Use the straw to slurp up the applesauce to see how it tastes.

Frogs

Feed the Frogs

Supplies

template—dragonfly, page 95
construction paper
party blowers
string
clothes hangers
hole punch

Skills

eye-hand coordination
oral motor
blowing
color concepts
vocabulary

Instructions for Teacher

1. Use the template to make dragonflies from three colors of construction paper.
2. Punch a hole in the top of each dragonfly and tie a piece of string on it. Suspend three dragonflies of different colors from each hanger.
3. Hold the hanger in front of the child so the dragonflies are at face level six to eight inches away.
4. Give the child a party blower. Explain that he should pretend to be a frog. The blower is the frog's tongue.

Instructions for Child

1. Blow your blower so it "catches" a dragonfly.
2. Tell what color the dragonfly is.
3. See how many times you can catch a dragonfly.

94   Animals

Dragonfly

Animals

Frogs at Home on a Lily Pad

Supplies

template–frogs
and lily pads, page 97

bright green, light green
and turquoise
construction paper

bright-colored
tissue paper

glue sticks

white glue

Skills

visual perception

copying a model

following directions

pasting

size concepts

vocabulary

Instructions for Teacher

1. For each frog and lily pad scene, you will need one 8½" x 11" sheet of turquoise construction paper for the background, one large lily pad, one small lily pad, one frog and several pieces of tissue paper for lily pad flowers.
2. Cut the tissue paper into two-inch square pieces.
3. Assemble a model for the children to copy. Use a glue stick to glue down the lily pads and frogs. Use white glue to attach tissue paper "flowers" to the lily pads.
4. Show the children the model. Tell them the background is the pond. Lily pads grow and bloom in the pond. Frogs like to swim in the pond and hop on the lily pads.
5. Demonstrate how to roll the tissue paper squares into balls using your thumb and fingertips.

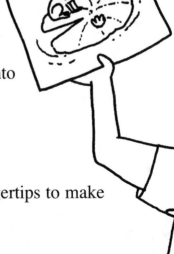

Instructions for Child

1. Glue the lily pads on the pond.
2. Roll the tissue paper between your thumb and fingertips to make flowers.
3. Glue the flowers to the lily pads.
4. Glue the frog on a lily pad.

Animals

Frogs and Lily Pads

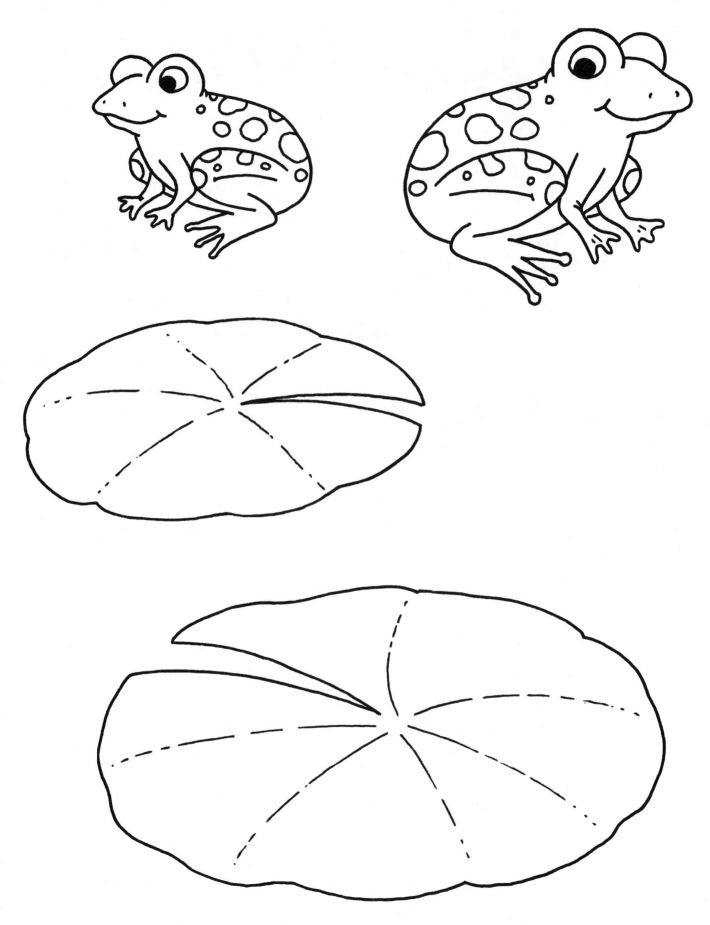

Animals

Lily Pad Float

Supplies

water table or plastic tubs

water

sponges

small objects
(counting bears or
baby food jar lids)

Skills

eye-hand coordination

grasp and prehension

tactile: wet/temperature

weight concepts

counting

vocabulary

Instructions for Teacher

1. Fill a water table or several plastic tubs with water. Float the sponges in the water to act as lily pads.
2. Explain that the sponges are lily pads floating in a pond. Children will see how much weight they can put on the lily pads before they sink.
3. Give each child a sponge and several small objects.

Instructions for Child

1. Place your lily pad sponge in the water. Carefully place the small objects one at a time on your "lily pad."
2. Tell the teacher which objects are heavy and which are light.
3. Count the number of objects it takes to sink your "lily pad."

Froggyland Game

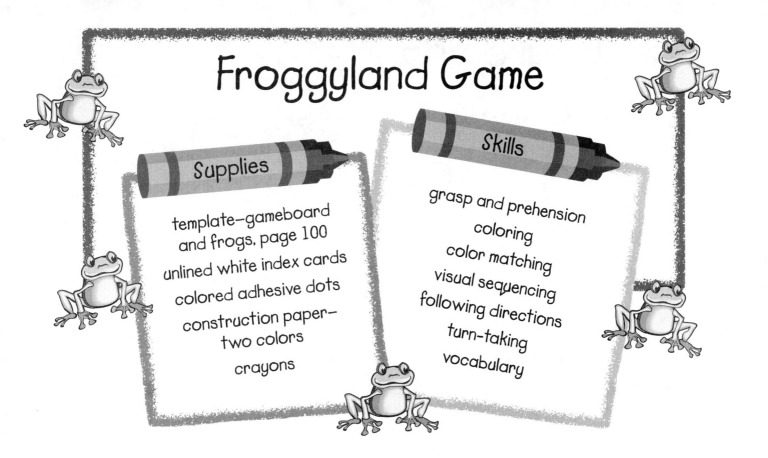

Supplies

template–gameboard
and frogs, page 100
unlined white index cards
colored adhesive dots
construction paper–
two colors
crayons

Skills

grasp and prehension
coloring
color matching
visual sequencing
following directions
turn-taking
vocabulary

Instructions for Teacher

1. Make a copy of the gameboard template for each child.
2. Cut the index cards in half lengthwise. Each child will need eight cards and eight colored adhesive dots (two each of red, blue, yellow and green).
3. Cut out two frogs per child from two different colors of construction paper to use as playing pieces (one for the child and one for the opponent).
4. Make a model gameboard and game cards to show the children. Color the gameboard in the sequence of red, blue, yellow and green. Stick the colored dots on the eight cards.
5. Give each child a gameboard, two frogs, eight index cards, eight dots (red, blue, yellow and green) and four crayons (red, blue, yellow and green).

Instructions for Child

1. Stick one colored dot on each of the eight index cards.
2. Color the circles on the gameboard with red, blue, yellow and green crayons until the path is completely colored. Color the lily pad green.
3. Game Rules: Each player gets a frog. Place the cards facedown. Pick a card and move your frog to the next circle of the color on the card. The next player takes a turn. The first frog on the large lily pad wins!

Gameboard and Frogs

Start

Animals

Leapfrog

Supplies

non-skid spots, or 10"-diameter construction paper circles, laminated and secured to the floor with masking tape

Skills

strength
balance and coordination
jumping and hopping
spatial awareness
motor planning
distance concepts
size concepts
vocabulary

Instructions for Teacher

1. Arrange non-skid spots or construction paper circles (lily pads) in a "frog path" on the floor spaced various distances apart, some close together and some farther apart. Make sure they are secured to the floor so the child doesn't slip while jumping. Place two spots side-by-side so the child has to jump with his feet apart to put one foot on each of the spots.
2. Demonstrate jumping from lily pad to lily pad along the path.
3. Explain that the children are little frogs jumping from lily pad to lily pad in their frog pond.

Instructions for Child

1. Stand on the first lily pad spot and jump from spot to spot until you reach the end of the path.
2. Make sure your feet land on the lily pad so you don't fall in the pond!
3. Tell the teacher which spots are close together, which are far apart and whether your jumps are small or big.

Variations

Vary the pattern of the spots for each child. After each child has a turn, have him or her rearrange the spots for the next child.

Pets

TLC10470 Copyright © Teaching & Learning Company, Carthage, IL 62321-0010

Puppy Class

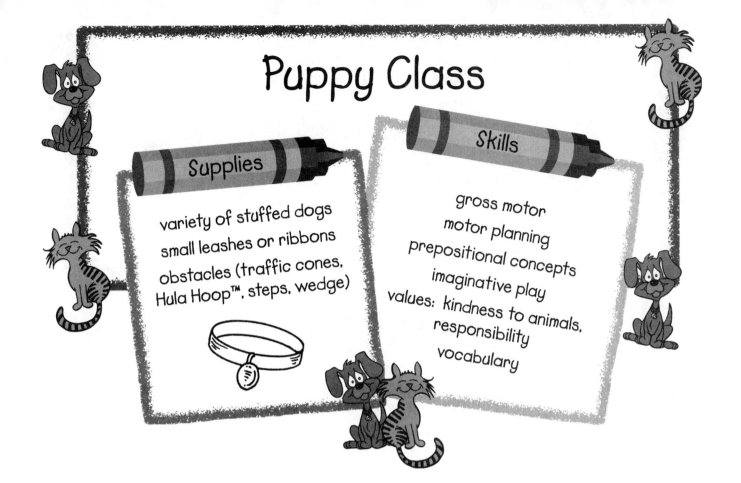

Supplies

variety of stuffed dogs
small leashes or ribbons
obstacles (traffic cones,
Hula Hoop™, steps, wedge)

Skills

gross motor
motor planning
prepositional concepts
imaginative play
values: kindness to animals,
responsibility
vocabulary

Instructions for Teacher

1. Set up an obstacle course for the children to walk their dogs through. (Example: Walk up a big wedge, up and down a step, through a Hula Hoop™ and around a traffic cone.)
2. Tell the children they are taking their puppies to puppy class to teach them how to walk on a leash.
3. Demonstrate by taking a stuffed puppy on a leash through the obstacle course, modeling how to talk to the puppy ("Come, puppy!" and "Stay, puppy!").
4. After everyone has had a turn, encourage them to talk about their own pets.

Instructions for Child

1. Choose one of the stuffed puppies on a leash and give your puppy a name.
2. Take your puppy through the obstacle course. Tell your puppy what to do at each station ("Up the step, puppy!").
3. Be kind and gentle, pet the puppy and be sure to tell him he is doing a good job!

Paw Print Path

Supplies

template–paw prints, page 105

scissors

dice

clear, self-adhesive plastic or laminating materials

Skills

mobility

jumping

number concepts

counting

turn-taking

vocabulary

Instructions for Teacher

1. Make 20 copies of the paw print template. Laminate them or cover them with clear, self-adhesive plastic. Cut out the paw prints.
2. Arrange the paw prints in a straight line on the floor approximately 12 inches apart. Tape them down so they don't slip.
3. Show children how to throw a die, count the spots and take that number of jumps along the paw print path. Explain that they will take turns with partners to see who can get to the end of the path first.
4. Have two children start at the starting point.

Instructions for Child

1. First child: Throw the die, tell what number you rolled and jump with your feet together that number of paw prints, counting them out loud.
2. Second child: Throw the die and jump on the path in the same way.
3. Take turns until one of you reaches the end of the path.

104   Animals

Paw Prints

Hidden Pets

Supplies

5 plastic bowls

small plastic animals
(some pets, some not pets)

scooter board or turtle

masking tape

Skills

balance and coordination

strength

naming

categorizing

vocabulary

Instructions for Teacher

1. Mark a starting point on the floor with a masking tape line. Put the scooter board or turtle behind the line.
2. Place the bowls upside down on the floor in a straight line at three-foot intervals.
3. Place one plastic animal under each bowl. Some of the animals should be pets such as a dog or a cat, and some should be wild animals such as an elephant or a zebra. The children will ride down the path and find the hidden animal under each bowl. They will name the animal and say whether it is a pet or not.
4. Change the hidden animals several times throughout the activity to challenge the children and vary their vocabulary.

Instructions for Child

1. Sit on the scooter board at the starting line.
2. Ride to the first bowl and uncover the animal.
3. Name the animal and tell whether it is a pet or not.
4. After you have done this at all five bowls, ride back to the starting line.

Pet!

106   Animals

Dalmatian Spots

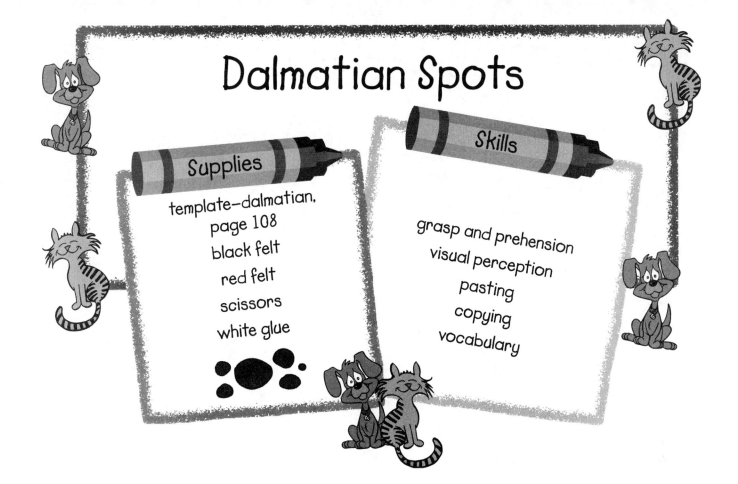

Supplies

template-dalmatian, page 108
black felt
red felt
scissors
white glue

Skills

grasp and prehension
visual perception
pasting
copying
vocabulary

Instructions for Teacher

1. Copy the dalmatian template for each child, and one for a sample.
2. Cut out a red felt hat and several black felt spots for each child.
3. Glue the spots and hat on the dog as a model to show the children.
4. Give each child a copy of the dalmatian template, a red felt hat, several black felt spots and glue.

Instructions for Child

1. Look at the dalmatian model. Make one like it to take home.
2. Glue the red hat and the black spots on your dalmatian.

Variations

Have the child cut out the dalmatian hat and the felt spots.

Dalmatian

Buster

Animals

Caring for Pets

Supplies

stuffed dogs and cats
plastic tub
towels
brushes
treats
toy stethoscopes, etc.
bandages
bench

Skills

pretend play
grooming
expressive language
values: kindness to animals, responsibility
vocabulary

Instructions for Teacher

1. Set up a pretend pet grooming area with stuffed dogs and cats, a tub, towels, brushes and treats and a veterinary clinic with stuffed dogs and cats, a bench, toy stethoscopes and other toy medical instruments, bandages and treats.
2. Tell the children they will be learning how to take care of pets.
3. Talk about grooming. Name the items in the pet grooming area. Name the items in the veterinary clinic area and discuss their uses. Emphasize the vocabulary.

Instructions for Child

1. Choose a stuffed animal and give it a name.
2. Go to the grooming area or the veterinary clinic with your pet. Play in that area until the teacher tells you to switch to the other area.
3. Talk about what you are doing with your pet and why.

Down on the Farm

Planting on the Farm

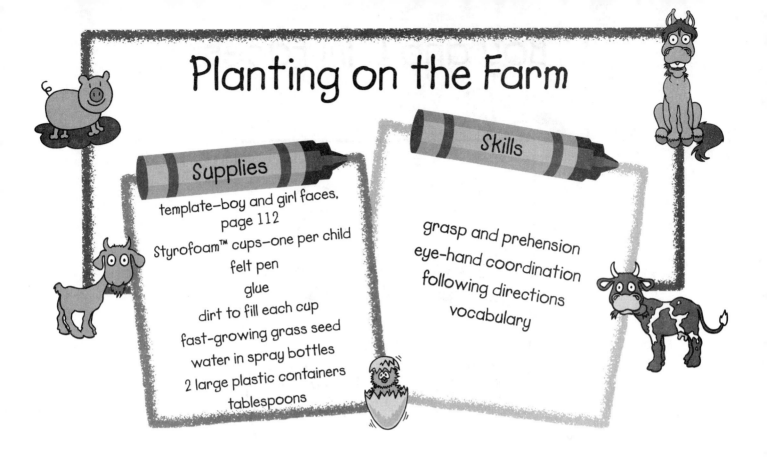

Supplies

template—boy and girl faces, page 112
Styrofoam™ cups—one per child
felt pen
glue
dirt to fill each cup
fast-growing grass seed
water in spray bottles
2 large plastic containers
tablespoons

Skills

grasp and prehension
eye-hand coordination
following directions
vocabulary

Instructions for Teacher

1. Copy and cut out the face templates.
2. Put dirt in a container with several table-spoons.
3. Place grass seed in a container and fill spray bottles with water.
4. Using a felt pen, mark a line on the inside of each cup to indicate a fill-line. Give each child a cup, a boy or girl face and glue.

Instructions for Child

1. Glue a boy or girl face on the side of the cup.
2. Fill the Styrofoam™ cup with dirt to the fill-line.
3. Sprinkle grass seed on the dirt, then cover it with a little more dirt.
4. Spray water over the seed. Water it every day.
5. Wait for the grass to grow and watch it become the child's hair.
6. Cut the "hair" if it grows too long.

Boy and Girl Faces

Animals

Are You My Mother?

Supplies

templates—mother and baby animals, pages 114-119

ball

masking tape

Skills

motor planning
eye-hand coordination
following directions
vocabulary

Instructions for Teacher

1. Cut out the mothers and babies separately from the templates. Attach the figures of mother animals to the wall at floor level.
2. Place a masking tape line six to eight feet from the figures. Place a ball near the spot.
3. Hold up the pictures of baby animals for children to name. Have them roll the ball to the mother of each baby.

Instructions for Child

1. Sit on the tape line.
2. Wait for the teacher to hold up a baby animal. Name the animal.
3. Roll the ball to the picture of the baby's mother and name it.

Variations

Match pictures of things that go together or things that are opposite.

Mother and Baby Animals

Animals

Mother and Baby Animals

Mother and Baby Animals

Animals

Mother and Baby Animals

Mother and Baby Animals

Animals

Mother and Baby Animals

Animals

What's on the Farm?

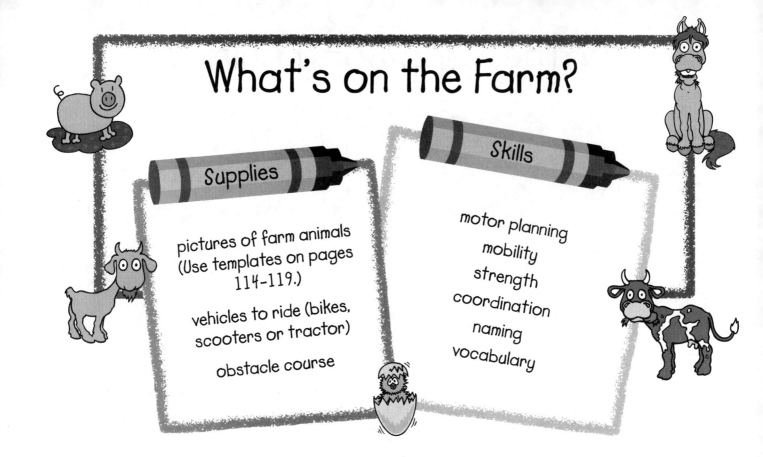

Supplies

pictures of farm animals
(Use templates on pages
114–119.)

vehicles to ride (bikes,
scooters or tractor)

obstacle course

Skills

motor planning
mobility
strength
coordination
naming
vocabulary

Instructions for Teacher

1. Create an obstacle course using whatever objects are available, making sure there is room between the objects for the child to maneuver a vehicle around, between, through, etc. End the course near the starting line.
2. Set a starting point where the child is to begin the course.
3. Place pictures of animals along the obstacle course. The pictures can be attached to objects or lying on the floor (out of the way of vehicles).

Instructions for Child

1. Choose a vehicle to ride and begin at the starting point.
2. Ride through the obstacle course stopping at every picture. Name the animal picture and make the animal noise.
3. Continue on the course until you get back to the starting point.

Moo!

Fun on the Farm with Horseshoes

Supplies

plastic horseshoes

plastic stakes/stand

masking tape

Skills

eye-hand coordination

motor planning

strength

underhand throwing

vocabulary

Instructions for Teacher

1. Create a horseshoe pit by driving stakes into the ground and clearing the area around the stakes.
2. Place a tape line on the floor four to six feet away from the stakes. Put horseshoes behind the line.
3. Demonstrate the proper way to hold and throw a horseshoe, being sure that the elbow is extended at the time of release.
4. Explain what a "ringer" and a "leaner" are (see below).

Instructions for Child

1. Stand behind the tape line and pick up a horseshoe. Throw the horseshoe at the stake, trying to get a ringer or a leaner.

ringer—the horseshoe is around the stake

leaner—the horseshoe is leaning against the stake

Clothespin Farm

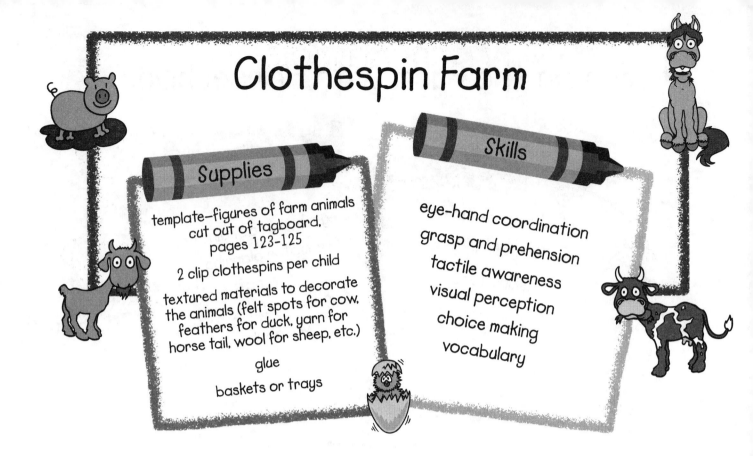

Supplies

template–figures of farm animals cut out of tagboard, pages 123-125

2 clip clothespins per child

textured materials to decorate the animals (felt spots for cow, feathers for duck, yarn for horse tail, wool for sheep, etc.)

glue

baskets or trays

Skills

eye-hand coordination

grasp and prehension

tactile awareness

visual perception

choice making

vocabulary

Instructions for Teacher

1. Place figures of farm animals on the table.
2. Separate the different textures and clothespins into baskets or trays.
3. Ask the child to name each animal and decide what texture best suits the animal.

Instructions for Child

1. Select an animal, two clothespins and the texture you think should go on it.
2. Glue the texture onto the animal. Clip on two clothespins for legs.

122   Animals

Farm Animals

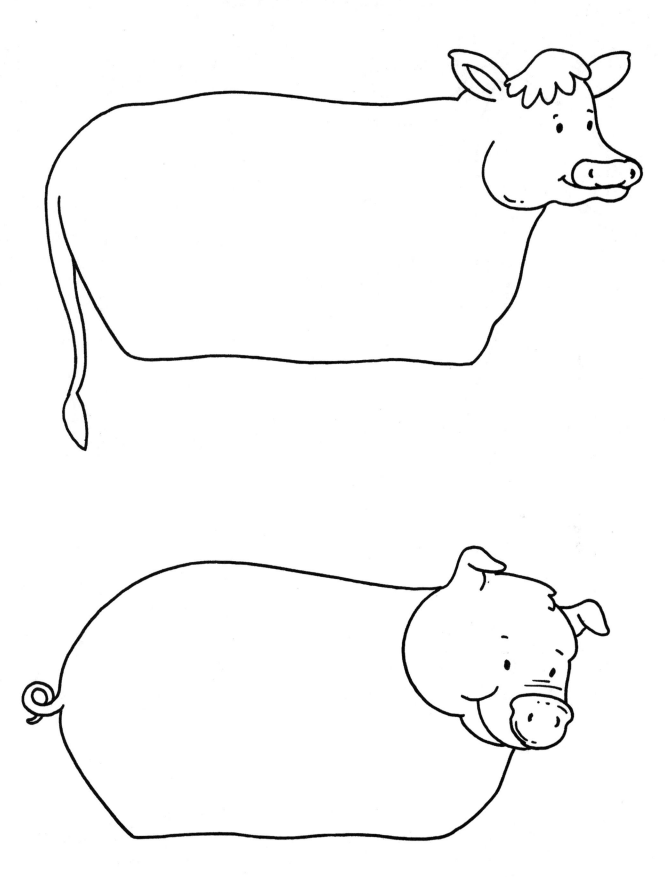

Farm Animals

Animals

Farm Animals

Feather Fun

(And you thought feathers were only for birds!)

TLC10470 Copyright © Teaching & Learning Company, Carthage, IL 62321-0010

Feather Float

Supplies

variety of colored feathers
variety of thematic objects
basket

Skills

eye-hand coordination
visual tracking
grasp and release
prepositional concepts
vocabulary

Instructions for Teacher

1. Mark a place on the floor for the child to stand.
2. Place colored feathers in a basket next to the colored spot.
3. Place a variety of thematic objects around the standing marker approximately one foot away.

Instructions for Child

1. Take a brightly colored feather from the basket and name its color.
2. Stand on the standing marker.
3. Raise your hand above your head and drop the feather.
4. Watch the feather float to the ground.
5. Name the item the feather lands on or falls near.
6. Answer questions your teacher asks about the item.

Variations

Include objects that have colors, numbers or letters to work on pre-readiness skills.

Anything Can Happen

Light as a Feather

Supplies

variety of colored feathers

pictures or objects

masking tape

basket

Skills

eye-mouth coordination

visual tracking

oral motor

prepositional concepts

vocabulary

Instructions for Teacher

1. Put thematic pictures or objects on the floor at the opposite side of the table from where the child is sitting.
2. Place colored feathers in a basket.
3. Put masking tape on the table as a starting line.

Instructions for Child

1. Take a brightly colored feather from the basket and name it.
2. Put the feather on the masking tape line and blow it across the width of the table until it falls to the floor.
3. Go to the other side of the table and see what picture or object the feather landed on or near.
4. Answer questions the teacher asks about where the feather landed.

Variations

Include objects that are weighed differently—a Ping-Pong™ ball, cotton ball or a small tissue paper ball.

Birds of a Feather . . .

Supplies

template–birds
without tails, page 130

variety of
colored feathers

egg stickers

glue

Skills

eye-hand coordination
grasp and prehension
finger isolation
pasting
tactile awareness
vocabulary

Instructions for Teacher

1. Prepare one copy of the bird picture template for each child and one for a model.
2. Assemble a model by gluing feather tails on the birds and placing egg stickers in the grass.
3. Put glue, feathers and stickers on the table.
4. Give each child a copy of the template. Show the children the completed model and have each make one like yours.

Instructions for Child

1. Count out six feathers. Glue two feathers on each bird for a tail.
2. Peel off the egg stickers using your index finger and thumb.
3. Put the eggs in the grass.

Variations

Color the birds or draw bugs and worms. Have the child duplicate a pattern designed by the teacher (AB or ABC) when placing the eggs in the grass.

Birds Without Tails

Anything Can Happen

Feeding Our Feathered Friends

Supplies

variety of colored feathers

ladder or step stool

candy worms in a dish

large roll of butcher paper
(green for leaves and
brown for trunk)

bird's nest (paper or basket)

bird (paper or stuffed)

Skills

motor planning

balance/coordination

strength

sensory: taste

color concepts

vocabulary

Instructions for Teacher

1. Make a large paper tree and place it on the wall. Put a bird nest with a bird in it on the tree.
2. Place a step stool or ladder next to the tree.
3. Put candy worms in a dish next to the stool or ladder.

Instructions for Child

1. Take a candy worm from the dish and tell what color it is.
2. Climb up the stool or ladder with a candy worm in hand. (Close teacher supervision is required.)
3. Reach out and feed the worm to the bird.
4. Once the bird has "eaten" the worm, become a bird and eat the worm, too. Yum! Yum!

Variations

Ask the child to find a specific color worm in the dish.

Bird-Watching

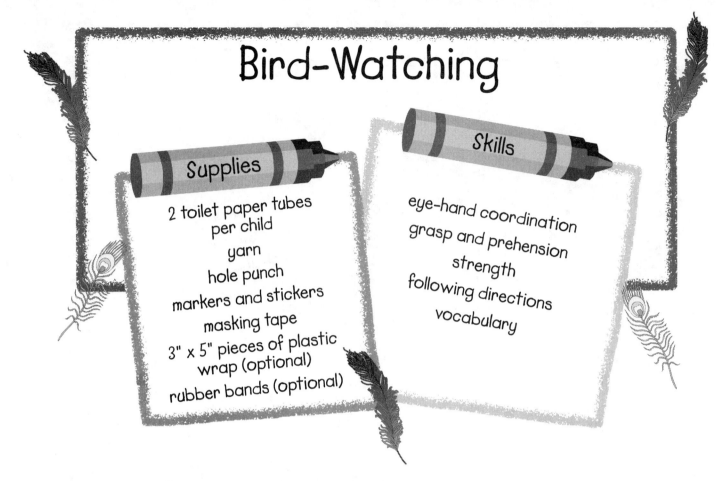

Supplies

2 toilet paper tubes per child
yarn
hole punch
markers and stickers
masking tape
3" x 5" pieces of plastic wrap (optional)
rubber bands (optional)

Skills

eye-hand coordination
grasp and prehension
strength
following directions
vocabulary

Instructions for Teacher

1. Tape two toilet paper tubes together side by side. Give one pair to each child.
2. Cut a 16-inch piece of yarn for each child.
3. Put all other materials on the table for the child to use.
4. Tell the children they are going to make binoculars to go bird-watching.

Instructions for Child

1. Decorate a pair of tubes using markers and stickers.
2. Punch a hole on the outside of one tube and another hole on the outside of the other tube, on the same end. The teacher will help you with this.
3. Make a strap for the binoculars by threading yarn through each hole and tying it.
4. For "lenses," put a piece of plastic wrap over the end of each tube and hold it on with a rubber band.
5. Go look at some birds with your binoculars!

Tube Day

Tube Bowling

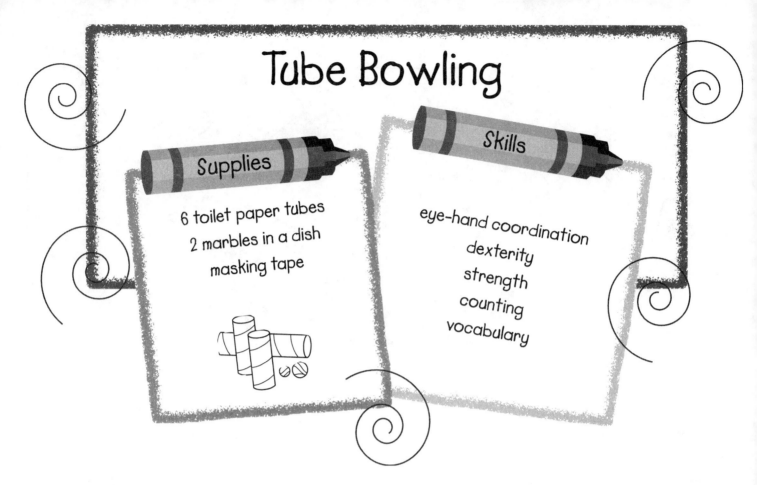

Supplies

6 toilet paper tubes
2 marbles in a dish
masking tape

Skills

eye-hand coordination
dexterity
strength
counting
vocabulary

Instructions for Teacher

1. Place the toilet paper tubes on end in rows of three tubes, two tubes and one tube like bowling pins on the floor.
2. Mark a start line with tape and put a dish with two marbles in it by the line.
3. Demonstrate how to flick a marble with the middle finger and thumb toward the tube.

Instructions for Child

1. Go to the tape line and lie on your tummy.
2. Pick up a marble. Use your middle finger and thumb to flick it at the tubes and knock them down. Take the second marble and do the same thing to knock down more tubes.
3. Count the number of tubes you knocked down and the number of tubes that are standing.

Variations

Color, number or letter the tubes to work on other pre-readiness skills.

Tube Car Race

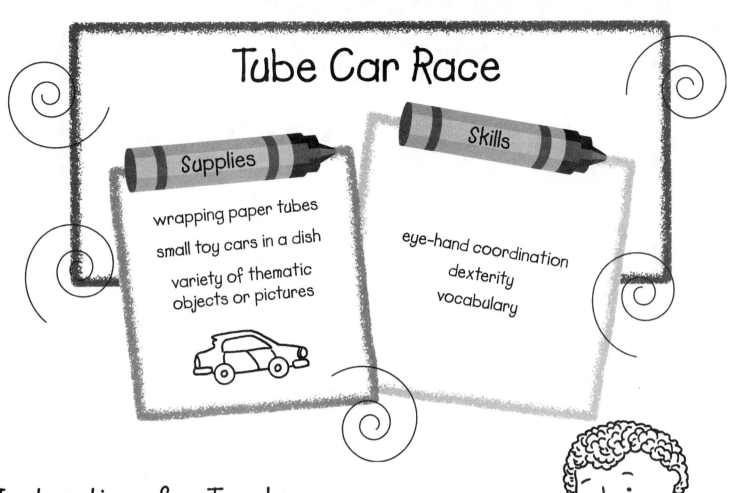

Supplies

wrapping paper tubes

small toy cars in a dish

variety of thematic objects or pictures

Skills

eye-hand coordination

dexterity

vocabulary

Instructions for Teacher

1. Mark an X on the floor with masking tape and place a variety of thematic objects or pictures in a circle around it approximately five feet away.
2. Put the tubes and a dish of small toy cars next to the X.
3. Be ready to provide prompts as the children tell about the objects or pictures their cars land on.

Instructions for Child

1. Stand on the X, select a small colored car and name the color to the teacher.
2. Hold a wrapping paper tube on an angle with one end touching the floor with one hand. Send the car rolling down the tube with the other hand.
3. Name the object or picture the car landed on or near.
4. Tell the teacher two things about the object or picture.

Tube Drop

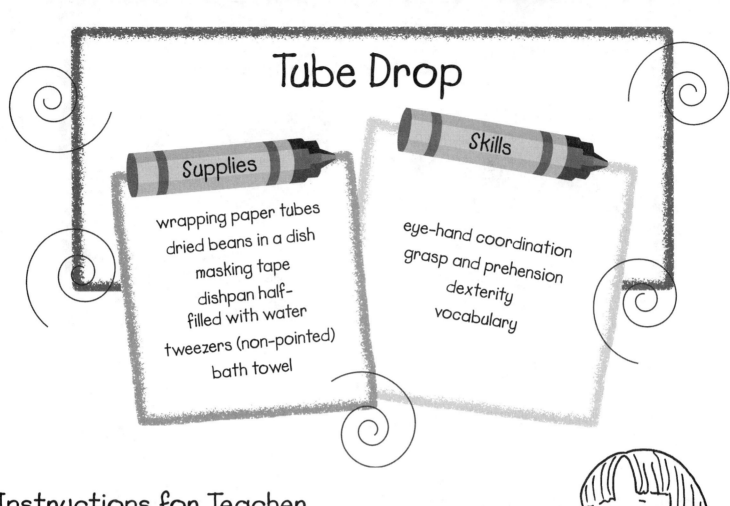

Supplies

wrapping paper tubes
dried beans in a dish
masking tape
dishpan half-
filled with water
tweezers (non-pointed)
bath towel

Skills

eye-hand coordination
grasp and prehension
dexterity
vocabulary

Instructions for Teacher

1. Place a dishpan half-filled with water on the floor with a towel under it. Place the wrapping paper tubes next to the pan.
2. Demonstrate how to use the tweezers (using an index finger and thumb) to pick up a dried bean from the bowl.
3. Show the child how to hold the wrapping paper tube at an angle right above the water and drop a bean through the tube.

Instructions for Child

1. Pick up a bean with the tweezers. Release the bean down the tube you are holding at an angle.
2. Wait for the bean to hit the water. Listen for the splash, then watch the ripple in the water.
3. Repeat this activity until the teacher tells you to stop.

Variations

Send objects of different sizes and weights down the tube to determine how they impact the splash and ripples.

The Balancing Tube Act

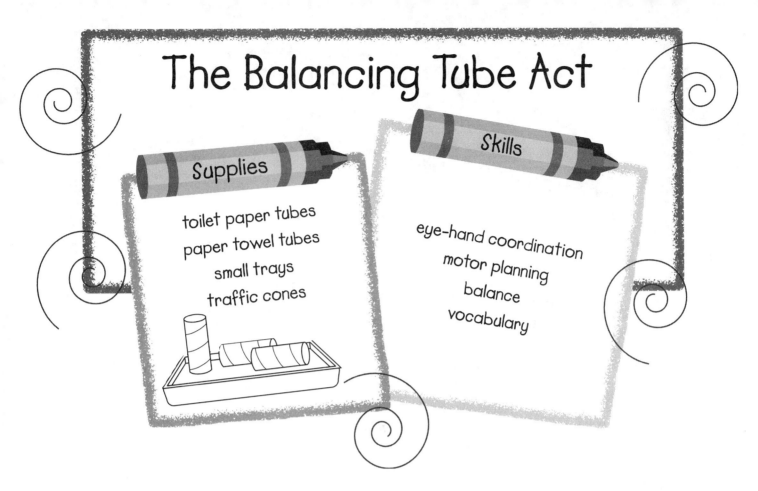

Supplies

toilet paper tubes
paper towel tubes
small trays
traffic cones

Skills

eye-hand coordination
motor planning
balance
vocabulary

Instructions for Teacher

1. Place two cones approximately five feet apart from each other.
2. Set out a small tray and several tubes near each cone.
3. Mark a starting point at the first cone.

Instructions for Child

1. Stand on the starting point. Pick up a tray and a tube.
2. Place the tube in an upright position on the tray.
3. Hold the tray with both hands and walk around the cones and back to start. Don't let the tube fall over!

Variations

Increase the challenge by:
    placing several tubes on the tray,
    holding the tray with only one hand,
    using a paper towel tube vs. a toilet paper tube,
    walking with the tube on the back of a hand.

Musical Tubes

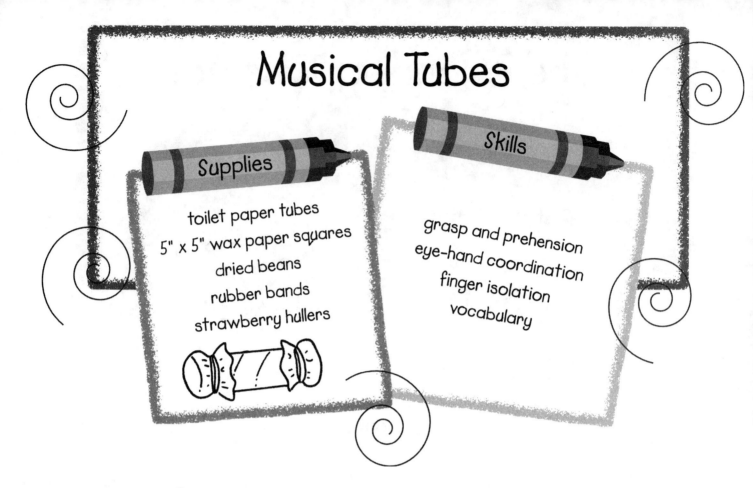

Supplies

toilet paper tubes
5" x 5" wax paper squares
dried beans
rubber bands
strawberry hullers

Skills

grasp and prehension
eye-hand coordination
finger isolation
vocabulary

Instructions for Teacher

1. Place the supplies on the table.
2. Demonstrate how to use the strawberry huller with a thumb and index finger to pick up beans.

Instructions for Child

1. Fasten one square of wax paper over one end of a toilet paper tube with a rubber band.
2. Use a strawberry huller with your index finger and thumb to place 10 beans into the tube.
3. Count the beans as you put them in.
4. Cover the open end of the tube with another wax paper square and a rubber band.
5. Shake your new musical instrument!

Balls, Bags & Blankets

Catch a Can

Supplies

clean soup can (open at one end) for each child

1 golf ball for every two children

masking tape

Skills

eye-hand coordination

visual tracking

turn-taking

following directions

vocabulary

Instructions for Teacher

1. Put two rows of tape parallel to one another on the floor approximately six feet apart (length of tape is determined by the number of children). On each row of tape place a sticker every two feet. The stickers should be directly across from one another.
2. Make sure the open end of the can has no sharp edges.
3. Divide children into two equal groups. Have each child kneel on a sticker, facing his or her partner.
4. Give each child a can. Give one of the partners a golf ball.
5. Demonstrate how to "send" and "catch" a ball using the can. With a forward movement of the arm, "send" the golf ball, rolling it out of the can toward the partner. The receiving partner scoops the ball into the can, then sends it back to the partner.

Instructions for Child

1. Send and catch the ball in the can with your partner.
2. Do not touch the ball with your hands.

Bag Walking

Supplies

paper or cloth bags with handles (grocery bag with handles, large tote bag or pillowcase)

traffic cone

Skills

coordination
balance
motor planning
vocabulary

Instructions for Teacher

1. Mark a starting point and place a cone approximately 30 feet apart.
2. Demonstrate to the child how to bag walk, placing both feet inside the bag, grabbing the handles and slowly walking.

Instructions for Child

1. Stand on the colored spot.
2. Put your feet in the bag, hold the handles and carefully walk around the cone back to the starting point.

Variations

Add more challenging skills when walking is mastered: walking sideways, backwards, faster or hopping.

Caution! Close supervision is recommended. Hold on to children who have poor balance.

Blanket Blast

Supplies

twin-sized blanket

obstacle course
(boxes, blocks, chairs
or cones)

Skills

coordination
strength
endurance
"heavy work"
motor planning
vocabulary

Instructions for Teacher

1. Mark a starting point on the floor. Place a blanket beside it.
2. Set up an obstacle course, leaving lots of room between the obstacles so a child being dragged on a blanket can move easily in, out and between the obstacles without knocking anything over.
3. Assign each child a partner according to size and strength.

Instructions for Child

1. One of you sit on the blanket and your partner will pull you on the blanket through the obstacle course. Sit in the center of the blanket and hold on while your partner pulls you around and back to the starting spot.
2. When you finish, change places with your partner so you each have an opportunity to pull and to ride.

Note: An adult should be available to assist with the pulling. This activity should be done only on a smooth surface.

Scoop Ball

Supplies

scoops (made from clean empty milk jugs)

whiffle balls

Skills

eye-hand coordination
motor planning
throwing
catching
vocabulary

Instructions for Teacher

1. Divide children into pairs according to skill level. Position them a few feet apart facing each other.
2. Give each child a scoop and one of the partner a whiffle ball.
3. Demonstrate "scooping" by placing the ball inside the scoop and moving the arm in an underhand throwing motion and sending the ball to the partner.
4. The receiving partner holds the scoop out with the open side facing up to catch the ball. **Note:** Letting the ball bounce once allows the child receiving the ball to better motor plan his movements for a catch in the scoop.

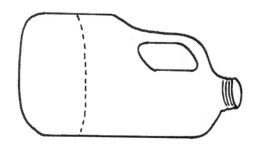

Scoops can be made from half-gallon milk jugs. Lay the milk jug on its side with the handle facing up. Cut the bottom off the jug, leaving the handle intact.

Anything Can Happen 143

Hula Ball Bounce

Supplies

Hula Hoop™
balls

Skills

eye-hand coordination
motor planning
throwing
catching
vocabulary

Instructions for Teacher

1. Divide children into pairs according to their ability to catch. Stand them across from each other with a Hula Hoop™ between them.
2. Give a ball to each set of partners.

Instructions for Child

1. Pick up the ball and bounce it once into the Hula Hoop™. Your partner will catch it and bounce it back to you.
2. Keep bouncing and catching the ball.

Variations

Change the size of the ball or the size of the Hula Hoop™, bounce the ball more than one time or change partners.

Note: Avoid using hard balls as children are sometimes fearful of trying to catch them.